KNITTING
BASICS

KNITTING
BASICS

A step-by-step course for first-time knitters

TRACEY LORD

CICO BOOKS
LONDON NEW YORK

Published in 2015 by CICO Books
An imprint of Ryland Peters & Small Ltd
20–21 Jockey's Fields, London WC1R 4BW
341 E 116th St, New York, NY 10029

www.rylandpeters.com

10 9 8 7 6 5 4 3 2 1

A CIP catalog record for this book is available from the
Library of Congress and the British Library.

ISBN: 978 1 78249 194 1

Printed in China

Editor: Marie Clayton
Pattern checkers: Susan Horan and Marilyn Wilson
Designer: Alison Fenton
Photographer: Penny Wincer
Flat shot photographer: Martin Norris
Stylist: Kiki Tse
Illustrator: Stephen Dew

Art director: Sally Powell
Production controller: David Hearn
Publishing manager: Penny Craig
Publisher: Cindy Richards

Contents

Introduction

Knitting is an ancient but perpetually popular craft. From its humble beginnings as a necessary and cheap method of making warm, durable clothing, to its development into a respectable drawing-room pastime for genteel ladies, knitting has seen numerous revivals—some born of thrift and necessity, others from a trend for handcrafted design. The most recent resurgence seems to be enduring—perhaps because in our busy, stressful lives, taking precious time out to make something is so very good for our souls. What remains a constant, however, is the fact that the simple act of being able to create something unique and wonderful from sticks and a ball of yarn has irresistible appeal and is almost alchemy to those who don't know how to do it! What could be better than immersing yourself in a mindful and satisfying pursuit while at the same time producing a beautiful, well-made treat for yourself or a loved one?

This book aims to give you a good understanding of all the basic techniques you will need to be able to tackle most knitting patterns. Each workshop has step-by-step instructions and illustrations, and every project only uses skills already covered earlier in the book. We've included practice swatches in the workshops so that you can really master the skills before you move on to the project that follows. The projects themselves are a mixture of "quick-to-make" and more involved accessories, garments, and pieces for your home. I hope you'll want to make them all!

Throughout the book I encourage you to keep examining your knitting, and noting certain properties about each type of fabric. By helping you to develop a wider perspective on what you are making—rather than just slavishly following instructions without understanding *why* certain stitches are called for—I hope you will develop enough confidence to eventually be able to create your own designs.

My art-teacher mother taught me to knit, in the same way that her own mother, a weaver, had taught her, and my first piece was, inevitably, a terribly misshapen scarf for my teddy bear. Yet it gave me a love of making and, years later, I now find it impossible to sit without having something to make in my hands, and still get very excited at the start of every new project. Knitting is addictive and immensely absorbing, a craft that crosses all boundaries and produces beautiful, sustainable, treasured pieces. I hope that you too will discover the sheer joy of knitting and gain the same lifelong enthusiasm and passion for knitting that I still enjoy.

How to use this book

Section 1: Getting started

In this section you will find the basics and background information you need to know before you start. There is advice on what type of yarns to choose, and which ones work best for particular projects; we also take a look at what all the information on the yarn ball band actually means. Next, there is guidance about types of knitting needle and suggestions for other bits of useful equipment that will help your knitting go smoothly.

Following this we look at some different ways to hold your needles and yarn; it's essential that you learn to do this properly so that your knitting comes out evenly, so there are plenty of helpful illustrations to guide you in this section. Then we cover how to cast on stitches and how to bind (cast) them off, and we also discuss the difference between knitting back and forth in rows, or in continuous rounds.

Next we look at the more technical aspects of knitting. There is a section about gauge (tension) and why it is so important, and you are shown how to make a gauge (tension) square so that you are ready to do this before tackling your first project. Finally, there's guidance to demystify all the terminology you might see at the start of a knitting pattern, including some common abbreviations. With all that information under your belt, you'll then be ready to make a start on the workshops and projects.

Section 2: Workshops and Projects

In this section you'll find a total of 20 workshops, each covering at least one new skill along with a project to put it into practice. There are step-by-step instructions and illustrations, and each workshop builds on the ones before it. Our first workshop will take you through the basic knit stitch and get you practicing casting on and binding (casting) off, before the first project pulls it all together into an easy-to-work piece.

Beyond this, we will look at how to combine knit and purl stitches to create textural effects, different ways to increase and decrease the number of stitches on your needles, how to work with more than one color, crossing stitches to create decorative cables, techniques to make secure tiny holes to create a lace pattern, knitting using beads, and various ways to embellish your pieces after they are complete.

If you are completely new to knitting, I suggest you follow the workshops in the order in which they occur. If you are brushing up your skills then you might prefer to find a workshop that teaches a skill you are less familiar with. Whatever your skill level, I hope that this book will become a useful reference and offer a tempting set of projects to show off your new skills.

Getting started

Materials and tools

The real basics to get started on knitting are just needles and some yarn, but it will help to have some information about all the different options that are available. Using the right needles and yarn will make the learning process much easier and will help to ensure that the items you make will look good right from the start.

Yarns

A vast array of knitting yarns is on offer, and the number will only increase as new materials are invented. Your pattern should guide you as to what type and thickness of yarn to use, but if you do not have a pattern then the chart below will help you match yarn thickness to needle size.

When choosing a yarn, consider the purpose of the item. Children loathe scratchy sweaters so you would not choose rough wool for a baby jacket—something soft such as a cotton blend, soft acrylic, bamboo, or silk blend would produce a snuggly fabric. Similarly, soft cotton would not be suitable for formal socks because cotton has no elasticity and would soon become baggy—a specialist wool and nylon sock yarn has durability and stretch, making it a much better choice.

Standard Yarn Weight
Categories of yarn, gauge (tension) ranges, and recommended knitting needle sizes

Yarn weight symbol & category names	LACE 0	SUPER FINE 1	FINE 2	LIGHT 3	MEDIUM 4	BULKY 5	SUPER BULKY 6
Types of yarns* in category	10-count crochet thread, US fingering	UK 4-ply sock, baby, US fingering	baby, US sport	DK, US light worsted	US worsted, afghan, Aran	craft, rug, chunky	bulky, roving, UK super chunky
Gauge (tension) in stockinette (stocking) stitch to 4 in. (10 cm)	33–40** sts	27–32 sts	23–26 sts	21–24 sts	16–20 sts	12–15 sts	6–11 sts
Recommended needle in metric size range	1.5–2.25 mm	2.25–3.25 mm	3.25–3.75 mm	3.75–4.5 mm	4.5–5.5 mm	5.5–8 mm	8 mm and larger
Recommended needle in US size range	001 to 1	1 to 3	3 to 5	5 to 7	7 to 9	9 to 11	11 and larger

* The generic yarn-weight names in the yarn categories include those commonly used in the UK and US.
** Ultra-fine lace-weight yarns are difficult to put into gauge ranges; always follow the gauge given in your pattern for these yarns.

Animal-fiber yarns include wool, alpaca, llama, mohair, camel, and angora—or silk as a luxurious option. Most of these have little fibers that retain warmth, which is why they are so popular for winter garments. Plant-fiber yarns include cotton, linen, and bamboo, while viscose and rayon are also produced from plant-based raw materials. These yarns are more breathable and work well for light summer garments. Other man-made fibers include acrylic, Lurex, microfiber, nylon, elastene, polyester, and more sustainable new additions such as tencel. Many of these are easy to care for and—thanks to their ability to absorb bright dyes and be washed at high temperatures—are popular for children's garments. Add to this the various blends of fibers, and a dizzying choice is available to the knitter.

It is also important to consider the type of spin on the yarn you choose. Some yarns are very loosely spun, making them more challenging for beginners to work with. You may hear people refer to such yarns as "splitty"—when you work with them the fibers easily separate, so it becomes difficult to differentiate individual stitches on the needle. To check the spin of a yarn, gently twist the yarn in the opposite direction to the slant of the fibers so that it opens up into a group of straight strands. If this is very easy to do, and happens after only one or two twists, avoid this yarn when you are a beginner. Try to choose a yarn that is slightly more tightly spun; it will not split as easily and you'll be able to keep better control of your stitches.

Novelty spun yarns, such as those containing long fur fibers, mohair, ribbon tabs, bumpy slubs, or nobbles within the yarns, are also challenging for the beginner to work with. Save these yarns until you are confident with working basic stitches—they are fun to use and produce lovely textures, but again, it is harder to see individual stitches. Plain spun yarns are ideal for when you are starting out.

When buying yarn take care to buy enough of the same dye lot, even in so-called undyed or white. Dye lots and batches can vary enormously and it is heartbreaking to notice a visible, unintended stripe in your work after you have labored over it. Always err on the side of caution in terms of amount.

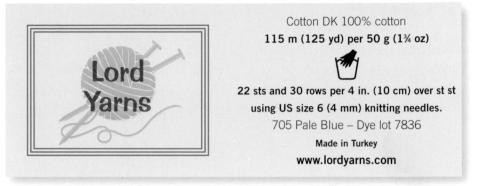

Cotton DK 100% cotton
115 m (125 yd) per 50 g (1¾ oz)

**22 sts and 30 rows per 4 in. (10 cm) over st st
using US size 6 (4 mm) knitting needles.**
705 Pale Blue – Dye lot 7836
Made in Turkey
www.lordyarns.com

Looking at yarn labels

When buying yarn you might shop in person at a local yarn store, department store, or at a craft fair, or you might prefer to shop online, where you can sometimes find a really good deal and a huge range but can't actually feel the yarn. Whichever you opt for, there should be standard information on either the ball band of the yarn or, if you are shopping online on the web page, which will help you choose the type and quantity to buy.

- **Brand name:** The name of the company that produced the yarn.
- **Fiber content:** Such as "55% wool/45% silk," which tells you how to care for the piece after you have made it, and which blocking method to use (see Workshop 1, Blocking, page 26) when making the piece.
- **Needle size:** The recommended size for best results—you might see either one size or a suggested range.
- **Gauge (tension) guide:** A suggestion of how many stitches and rows per 4 in. (10 cm) should be achieved by the "average" knitter, using the needle size given.
- **Yardage/meterage:** This tells you the length of yarn in one ball or hank. This is particularly important when substituting yarn, because your alternative may hold less or more yarn per ball so you might need more or fewer balls than the pattern states. Add up

the yardage of the number of balls given for the original yarn and then divide this figure by the yardage of the yarn you want to use as a substitute. The result, rounded up to the nearest whole number, tells you how many balls you need to buy.
- **Dye lot number:** This indicates which dye batch the yarn comes from. The color can vary in different batches, so with one-color items it's best to buy all the yarn from one dye batch.
- **Aftercare instructions:** you will often find guidance on how to wash and dry the completed garment.

Equipment

Knitting needles are available in plastic, metal, wood, and bamboo. Some people find metal needles harder on the hands, particularly those who suffer from arthritis. Bamboo and wood are said to help with this, although they can be more expensive.

Knitting needles come in many sizes: US size 0 (2 mm) is the smallest standard size and is very thin indeed, but needles go up to US size 50 (25 mm) and beyond for knitting with super-thick yarns or fabric strips. The most commonly used sizes, however, range from US size 3 (3.25 mm) for fingering (4-ply) yarn up to US size 10½ (6.5 mm) for bulky (chunky) yarn. US size 6 (4 mm) needles and a light worsted (DK) yarn is a good starting combination to learn with.

Straight needles come in various lengths—if you find it comfortable to knit lower on your body, with your needles toward your lap, then 12-in. (30-cm) long needles may be better for you, 14-in. (35-cm) long needles are useful for any style of knitting, and 16-in. (40-cm) needles are better for those who knit with one needle under one arm.

As well as straight needles there are circular needles, used for knitting in the round and frequently employed for knitting necklines and collars. These needles have a pair of shorter needle points connected by a length of nylon cord, and they are available in the same range of sizes as straight needles and a variety of cord lengths. Workshop 12 has more guidance about circular needles (see page 107).

Finally, there are sets of double-pointed needles, also known as "dpns." As the name implies, these have pointed tips at both ends and are used for specialist knitting, usually in the round for small tubular projects such as socks. Workshop 13 contains more guidance about working with dpns (see page 116).

Knitting needle conversion chart

UK/European and US needle sizes are differently labeled. If you have some very old needles, perhaps passed down from family members, they may have an older numbering system, so use the conversion chart or a needle gauge—which has labeled holes for all the common needle sizes—to work out the modern equivalent size.

US size	Metric size (mm)	Old UK/ Canadian
0	2.0	14
1	2.25	13
2	2.75	12
–	3.0	11
3	3.25	10
4	3.5	–
5	3.75	9
6	4.0	8
7	4.5	7
8	5.0	6
9	5.5	5
10	6.0	4
10½	6.5	3
–	7.0	2
–	7.5	1
11	8.0	0
13	9.0	00
15	10.0	000
17	12.0	–
19	16.0	–
35	19.0	–
50	25.0	–

Other equipment

You will also need many of the following items, depending on what you are making. It may not be necessary to buy everything at once—buy more specialist items as you need them.

Sharp scissors
Reserved for cutting fabric and yarn only: do not cut paper with these, as it will blunt them.

Tape measure
A tape with both inches and millimeters is ideal, so that you can convert measurements in the pattern if necessary.

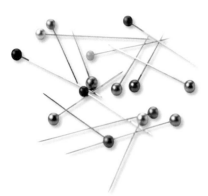

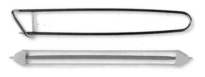

Pins
Rustproof, glass-headed, or T-headed quilters' pins to pin knitted pieces together. Bright-colored tops will help to avoid the pins getting lost in the knitted fabric.

Stitch markers
Little rings that slip on the needles to mark the start of rounds, or a particular place in the knitting.

Stitch holders
These are clips with a horizontal bar that you slip groups of stitches onto, and then clip closed, in order to save the stitches for later use.

Blunt-ended large-eyed darning needle
The blunt end will not split the yarn when sewing up.

Row counter
This is a small, tubular counter that fits on the end of your knitting needle; you click it round after each row.

Needle know-how

It's a good idea to store straight needles in a cloth roll or tube.

Circular needles and dpns are sometimes not labeled, so store them in their original packaging when not in use.

If you do find a mystery needle, a needle gauge can identify the size—find the hole your mystery needle fits snugly into (you should not have to ram it in, nor should it slip about), which will give you the size of your needle.

Cable needle
A small, double-pointed knitting needle for creating cable patterns.

Basic skills

Knitted fabric consists of a series of rows or rounds, with the yarn looping in and out of the previous row or round of loops. The basic stitches, and building blocks of all knitted fabrics, are knit stitch (see Workshop 1, page 22) and purl stitch (see Workshop 2, page 30). You will also need to know how to start off the knitting, known as casting on, and how to finish it off securely, so that it does not unravel, known as binding (casting) off.

Holding the needles and yarn

When you are ready to work, your elbows should be bent, with your arms carried roughly parallel to your waist or resting on your lap. If you choose to knit by the Continental, or German, method, then you control the yarn with your left hand; if you knit by the English method, then you will use your right hand to control the yarn.

How to hold the needles

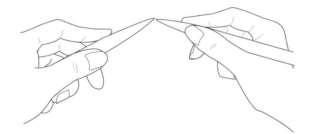

The needles are held between the thumb and forefinger like a pen, with the forefinger bent and the thumb resting on the middle portion of the forefinger. The remaining fingers curl round from below to support the needle.

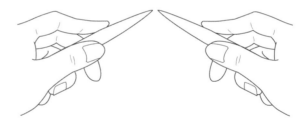

Alternatively, they can be held like a knife, with the main part of the needles resting inside between the fingertips and the palm of the hand.

Positioning the fingers

Try to keep your stitches and your fingertips close to the tips of the needles when you are working: this is much more efficient, because it means that your fingers and hands don't move as much for each stitch, which reduces the strain on your hands.

Some people like to keep one needle fixed, by tucking it under their right arm so that the right hand can concentrate on just working with the yarn. The left needle is held like a pen and moves as normal. This does give a lot of control but is not for everyone, although you may find it comfortable. It is common practice in the North of England and Scotland, and in some parts of Europe.

How to hold your yarn

Holding your yarn properly will make all the difference between good, even knitting and uneven, lumpy knitting. Your aim is to get the yarn flowing through your fingers at just the right pace, with just the right amount of tension applied to it. There is more information about the importance of gauge (tension) on page 18.

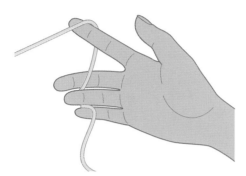 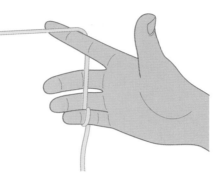

If you are right-handed you will probably want to hold and control your yarn in your right hand, which is known as the English method of knitting. Above are two suggested ways

of threading your yarn through your fingers to control it—try them both as you start to knit and see which feels most comfortable for you.

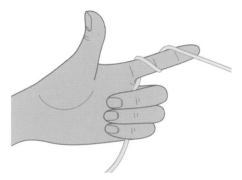 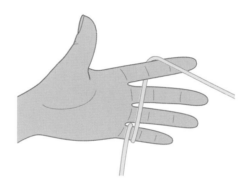

The Continental or German method of knitting is another alternative that is useful for left-handed people. Here are

two suggested ways of holding and controlling your yarn in your left hand.

Making a slip knot

A slip knot is the first loop that you put onto the needle to begin casting on in knitting.

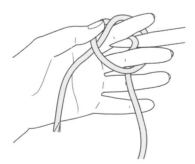 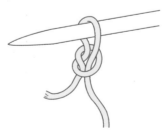

1 Make a slip knot by winding the yarn twice around the first two fingers of your left hand, then bend these fingers forward. Draw the rear thread through the front one to form a loop.

2 With the knitting needle in your right hand, slide the loop onto the needle. Remove your fingers, then pull the two ends to tighten the loop on the needle and create the first stitch. Keep the needle with the slip knot in your left hand.

Casting on

There are many ways to cast on stitches. Some give a particular quality to the edge of the work: they are either more elastic, so suited to things like stretchy cuffs, or give a rigid edge that is firm with added strength. As you progress you may want to investigate other methods (see Workshop 20, pages 163–165 for some alternative techniques.) The Internet will give you further options to try out. In the meantime, here is one very common and useful method of casting on that you can use for many of the projects in this book.

How to cast on (cable method)
This method makes a firm edge and uses two needles. It is given for the English method of knitting here.

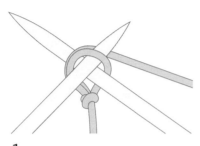 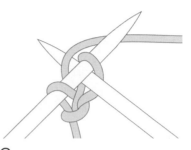

1 Keep the yarn at the back and insert the right needle into the slip knot, from front to back, as shown in the illustration. Wrap the yarn from the ball end round the tip of the right needle and pull downward gently on it.

2 Draw the tip of the right needle through the loop and, as you do so, nudge the yarn through the loop of the slip knot to make a new loop. Turn the needle a little and slip this new loop onto the left needle, in front of the slip knot, and off the right needle. You now have 2 stitches.

3 Now insert the tip of the right needle between the two stitches on the left needle. Wrap the yarn over the right needle, from left to right. Now draw the yarn through to form a loop as you did before, then transfer it to the left needle and off the right, as you did in step 2.

Repeat step 3 until you have created the desired number of stitches.

Rows and Rounds

Knitting is often worked in rows, or sometimes in rounds, and almost always from right to left. A row is a horizontal line of stitches that starts with the first stitch at one end and finishes with the last stitch at the other end. To continue working the next row you work on the other side of the knitting, from the first stitch to the last, and so on.

Knitting that is worked in rounds is always worked on the front, and on either circular needles (see Worksop 12, Knitting in the round, page 106) or a set of double-pointed needles (see Workshop 13, Double-pointed needles, page 116). There are projects that are made in rounds in later chapters of this book.

Binding (casting) off

To bind off (or cast off in the UK) means to make a finished, secure edge by closing the stitches. As with casting on, there are many methods of binding (casting) off, and you may choose to explore some of these as your skills develop.

How to bind (cast) off
This method is the most common way of finishing your knitting.

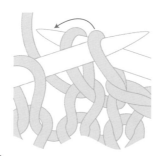

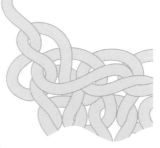

1 Knit the first two stitches of the next row as usual. Insert the tip of the left needle into the first stitch worked on the right needle, from left to right and at the front of the work. Lift this stitch over the last stitch on the right needle, and drop it off the tip. You will have one stitch remaining on the right needle.

2 Knit one more stitch from the left needle as normal so that you again have 2 stitches on the right needle, then repeat step 1 again.

3 Repeat until you have only one stitch left on the right needle and none on the left needle. Pull a long loop of yarn, then remove the right needle, cut the yarn, and thread the end through the loop, tightening it to close.

Gauge (tension)

Gauge (tension) is one of the most important aspects of successful knitting—it refers to the tightness of a knitted fabric and you should match yours to that given in the pattern you are working on so that your version of the item comes out the same size. This might sound hard to achieve, but all you need to know is how to make a gauge (tension) swatch, how to measure it, and what adjustments to make if your gauge (tension) does not match that in the pattern. This is even more crucial when you use a different yarn from that suggested in the pattern. The gauge (tension) in a knitting pattern, or on the ball band of yarn, is given as "X sts and Y rows to 4 in. (10 cm)." In a pattern it might also say "over pattern on US size XX (XX mm) needles," but if no stitch pattern is given it means worked in stockinette (stocking) stitch. Making sample swatches might seem a tedious process but it really is vital—even a small variation in gauge (tension) could produce a big difference in size over a larger piece—over-long sleeves, too short sweaters, or sagging shoulders can all be the product of incorrect gauge (tension). When you intend to invest your time and attention in knitting a piece, it's worth making sure it starts off right.

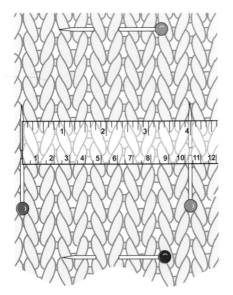

Making a gauge (tension) swatch

In order to find out what your gauge (tension) is, use the same size needles and cast on several more stitches than the given number then work in the given pattern until you have worked 4 in. (10 cm)—you can use a row counter to keep track of how many rows this takes. Bind (cast) off, and ideally block the swatch (see Workshop 1, page 26).

Make a note of how many rows you worked to make 4 in. (10 cm), then place a ruler across the swatch horizontally, taking care to follow a straight line of stitches, and count

how many there are over 4 in. (10 cm). Compare your figures to those of the given gauge (tension): if you have more stitches and rows, then work another swatch using one size bigger needles and check again. If you have fewer stitches and rows, work another swatch using one size smaller needles. Repeat this process until your gauge (tension) matches that in the pattern. When it does, use that size needle rather than what is given in the knitting pattern.

Reading a pattern

Throughout these workshops there are tips on how to read knitting a pattern and any charts. Knitting patterns follow a similar formula, although in this book we also list the skills used in each project, which is not standard knitting pattern information but is helpful to a beginner. Once you are used to the format of knitting patterns you will find that they become very familiar and will give the following information:

Materials: what yarn to use, how much to buy for each size, (again, using brackets if applicable), what size needles to use, any extra notions (haberdashery items) such as buttons, and extra equipment such as cable needles, stitch holders etc.

Sizing: Actual measurements of the finished piece and, in the case of garments, the measurements on the body they are intended to fit. Several sizes might be given in brackets; for example small(**medium**:large), so if you are following the medium size, use the information that comes first inside each set of brackets.

Gauge (tension): The number of stitches and rows to 4 in. (10 cm) when working a given pattern on the recommended needles. If you do not work to the stated gauge (tension) your piece will not be the given size, and garments may fit oddly or not at all.

Abbreviations: Details of what the abbreviations used in the pattern mean. These are usually standard (see right), but there may also be some special abbreviations that are only applicable to that pattern.

In addition there may also be one or more charts for color work or showing a texture pattern, with a key alongside to explain the symbols/colors used. Charts may show an entire garment piece or just a section, and should have markers along the bottom and side to help you count rows and stitches. There is much more information about charts in Workshops 11, 15, 16, and 17.

If you are making a garment or a complex piece you may also see a schematic diagram—either an outline showing the actual measurements at various points, or an assembly diagram.

Common abbreviations

alt	alternat(e)ing
beg	begin(ning)
C	cable (individual cable abbreviations are dealt with in Workshop 11)
cont	continu(e)ing
dec	decrease
dpn	double-pointed needle
foll	follow(ing)
inc	increase
inc 1	inc by knitting twice into stitch
k	knit
k2tog	knit 2 stitches together
M1	make 1 stitch increase
MB	make bobble
p	purl
p2tog	purl 2 stitches together
patt	pattern
rem	remain(ing)
rep	repeat
RS	right side
sl	slip
sl 1, k1, psso	slip 1 stitch, knit 1 stitch, pass slipped stitch over
ssk	slip 1 stitch, slip 1 stitch, knit the 2 slipped stitches together
st st	stockinette (stocking) stitch
st(s)	stitch(es)
tbl	through the back loop
tog	together
WS	wrong side
yf/yfwd	yarn forward
yo	yarn over the needle
yrn	yarn wrapped around the needle
[]	work instructions within brackets as many times as directed

Section 2

Workshops and projects

Workshop 1

Basic knit stitch

Now that you have got used to holding your yarn and needles and learned a basic cast-on method, you can start getting to grips with the basic knitting stitch. In this workshop you will learn how to make a knit stitch, how to bind (cast) off, how to weave in your loose tails and block your work after you have finished, and a quick method of joining up seams. With these skills you will be all set to complete Project 1, the Rustic Table Runner.

Knit stitch

This is the most fundamental of all the knitting stitches and forms the basis of most other knit structures. When you knit every row, the fabric you create is called garter stitch (see page 24). There are two standard ways to work a knit stitch: the English method and the Continental (German) method.

English method
Place the needle with the cast-on stitches in your left hand and the empty needle in your right. Thread your yarn around your right hand, as shown on page 15.

1 Insert the tip of the right needle into the first stitch on the left needle, going in at the front on the left of the stitch and through to the back on the right of the stitch.

2 Wrap the yarn from left to right over the tip of the right needle, so that it lies between the two needle tips and comes out and off to the right side.

3 Nudge the tip of the right needle toward the front so that the yarn is pulled through to the front to form a new loop. Make sure this new loop is securely on the right needle.

4 With the tip of the right needle, moving it to the right, push the stitch just worked off the tip of the left needle and gently tighten the new loop that now sits on the right needle. This is the first knit stitch.

Remembering the stitches

Here are two traditional rhymes to help you remember what to do when knitting in the English style: "Through the door, out the back, through the window and out comes Jack" or "In through the bunny hole, round the big tree; down through the bunny hole and out comes me!"

Repeat steps 1–4 for each stitch on the left needle, until this needle is empty. Count the stitches to check that you have not dropped any, or knitted twice into the same one by accident—both of these are very easy to do when you are learning. All you need to do is count the number of loops you have on your needle: in this case it should be the same number as you cast on.

To continue with the next row, put the now full right needle in your left hand and the now empty needle in your right hand—then work steps 1 to 4 again for each stitch.

Continental (German) method

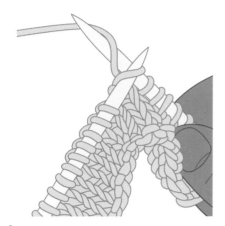 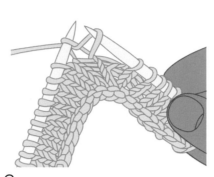 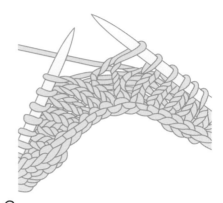

1 Again, start with the needle with the cast-on stitches in your left hand, and insert the tip of the right needle in the front of the first stitch, from left to right—exactly as with English knitting. The difference now is that you are holding and controlling the yarn in your left hand rather than your right. Tension the yarn with your left hand, at the back of the left needle, then move the tip of the right needle to pick up a loop of yarn.

2 Still using the tip of the right needle, draw the new loop of yarn through the original stitch on the left needle to form a new stitch on the right needle. Make sure that this new stitch is securely on the right needle.

3 Move the right needle toward the right and then gently push the original stitch off the left needle.

Repeat steps 1–3 until you have knitted all the stitches on the left needle. To make another row, swap the needles over and place the one full of stitches in your left hand, then begin again.

Working left handed

If you are left-handed, following conventional knitting patterns can be difficult at first: they are often written for the right-handed and rarely make reference to left-handed knitters. However, the Continental or German method of holding your yarn and needles should feel more comfortable because the "working" hand is the left hand in this method. Alternatively, place a mirror against all the illustrations, reversing them so that you can adapt them. Finally, check the many video tutorials available online for left-handed knitters: the advantage of these is that you can watch them over and over again, and knit along, until you have mastered a particular skill enough to be able to use conventional patterns with confidence.

Garter stitch

The fabric you create when you knit every row is called garter stitch. It is quite a wide and thick fabric that lies flat and is fairly durable. It has characteristic ridges and looks exactly the same on both sides.

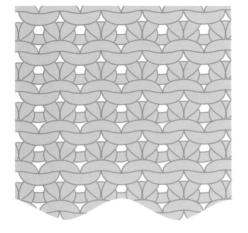

Counting rows and stitches in garter stitch fabric

Knit stitches are formed by yarn snaking up and down and in and out of loops, in a zigzag fashion. It is useful to know how to count rows, so that you can keep track of where you are in a pattern.

If you look at the diagram above, you will notice that in garter stitch there is a wavy pattern, then a row of indented Vs above, before another wavy pattern. One wavy row and one indented row of Vs together represent two rows of garter stitch. So you can count the wavy rows upward in twos, and if at the very top of your work there is a row of indented Vs, that is another one row to add on.

It is a very good idea, especially when you are a beginner, to count your stitches on the needle at very

regular intervals, to make sure you have not dropped any stitches or accidentally made any extra stitches. At this early stage, when you are still learning, do not worry too much about this: later workshops will show you how to put mistakes right, but for now try and notice any errors so that you can avoid making them again.

To count stitches on the needle, simply pick along the needle with your finger, moving the stitches along toward the tip a little (not too much, so that you don't stretch the stitches). Count in twos for speed.

To count the stitches along a row in garter stitch, each upper horizontal bar in the wavy line represents one stitch.

Finishing off your work

Many knitters find it daunting to spend time on the last stages of finishing off their work. After hours of carefully knitting the pieces, you might feel that to delay wearing or using your item any longer is the last thing you want to do! However, you could look at it from another perspective: after so many hours of careful work, it makes sense to spend just a little more time to make it look professional and well made. You will be even more proud of your efforts if you learn these techniques, and you will feel confident to give your work as a gift, safe in the knowledge that you have presented a beautifully made, durable piece that will be treasured for many years to come.

Weaving in yarn tails/ends

The first thing you need to do is deal with any loose yarn tails. As you become more competent you will be able to weave in some loose yarn tails as you work, reducing the need to devote time to it at the end. However, there will inevitably be some to deal with when you have finished, so this technique will always be useful. It takes its name from the "weaving" motion worked as you sew the yarn tails in and out of the stitches on the wrong side.

You will need a blunt-ended darning needle with a large eye—these are sometimes called "knitter's needles" or "yarn needles" and are often sold in pairs, one large and one smaller. A blunt-ended needle will not split the stitches into individual strands as you sew, which would make sewing much more difficult and produce a weak, untidy seam. You will also need small, sharp scissors.

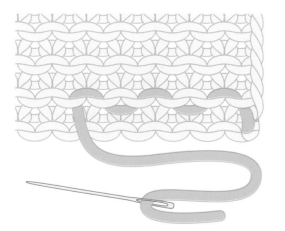

Take a yarn end and thread it into the needle. With the wrong side of the work facing you, follow along one row of horizontal stitch "bars"—this might be on the last/first row, or in the middle of the piece; wherever the yarn tail occurs, work in the row alongside it. Sew up and down through this row, working the yarn in and out so that it snakes through the stitches, as shown above. Work about 4 in. (10 cm) of the tail in, and then trim off close to the work.

Keeping the elasticity

Be careful not too pull too tightly on the yarn tail as you work, otherwise you will pucker the knitting and may reduce the elasticity of the knitted fabric. If it feels a little tight, stretch the knitting out a little and the yarn tail should adjust appropriately.

Where possible, try to weave in the yarn tails along seams, where they will be least visible. If you can't do this, then work as close to the seam as you can, and try to weave into an area of the same color as the tail.

Smooth and silky yarns need to be woven in for more stitches than coarser or woolen yarns do, because the latter have little hairs that grip and hold the tails in place. Working back on yourself as you stitch also helps stop the tails from slipping out.

Blocking

You will often see a reference in knitting instructions and patterns to blocking your work, which is a technique that allows you to adjust, straighten out, or re-shape your pieces before you sew them up. It is done after you have woven in loose yarn tails. Some knitters loathe blocking; it does take a little time, but the results can truly transform the look of your finished item. Again, do try to see it as a process that honors the amount of work you have put in, rather than a chore—it's like the icing on the cake!

The process involves dampening knitted (and also crocheted) pieces and pinning them out to the size or shape they are intended to be. It is particularly useful for achieving defined corners, accurate squares or rectangles, and to reduce the natural curl of some knitted fabrics. It is a fundamental necessity for items like fine lace shawls, which can look terrible when they come off the needles but are transformed into filigree works of art after blocking.

For larger pieces you will need a blocking board. You can buy ready-made blocking boards, but you can easily make your own, and the instructions for this are given in the tip box opposite. To learn the method, however, and to block the Rustic Table Runner project in this workshop, you can use a regular ironing board.

Basic blocking

This method of blocking requires no specialist equipment. It is suitable for use with most yarns, and especially those that have a mainly natural fiber content. Before you begin, check the ball band of your yarn for the fiber content. If your yarn is acrylic, or a wool-acrylic blend, then follow the instructions for cold water blocking. If you have used wool, cotton, silk, or linen, then use the steam method.

Equipment

- Water spray bottle OR steam iron, depending on method/fiber
- Ironing board with a reasonably thick level of padding
- Steel pins—glass-headed or, ideally, T-headed quilter's pins
- Ruler and tape measure

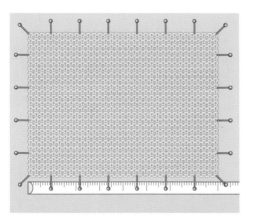

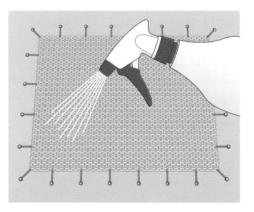

1 Lay your piece of knitting flat on the ironing board and begin to pin in place. Beginning with the corners, if there are any, place the pins to hold the edge of the knitting firm without distorting it. Pin so that only the pin head is above the ironing board—the longer part of the pin should be under the work. Use a ruler or tape measure to check that each side is the right measurement. Ease out the knitting and adjust the pins accordingly until you have pinned the piece out to the right size. Make sure that any right angles are correct, and that nothing looks distorted.

2 If you are using the cold water method (see above) spray the piece with cold water, using the spray bottle, until it is damp but not completely wet through. Pat down gently on the piece to make sure the entire piece has become damp, then leave it to dry naturally before removing the pins.

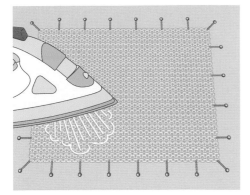

3 If you are using the steam method (see previous page), set the iron to the correct temperature for the yarn you have used—check the ball band if you are not sure. Hold the iron just below 1 in. (2.5 cm) above the surface of the pinned-out piece and steam constantly for one or two minutes. Do not allow the iron to touch the surface of the piece, because this will ruin the texture and pile of the yarn and may create an unwanted shiny surface. Once you have finished steaming, remove the iron and allow the piece to dry completely before removing the pins.

Repeat this for all the pieces of knitting you have prepared. In the case of small pieces, such as the project that follows, you may find you can fit several pieces on the board at a time, which greatly speeds up the process.

Making a blocking board

You will need a piece of hardboard approximately 40 in. (100 cm) square and a piece of thick batting (wadding) the same size. You will also need a piece of fairly sturdy, preferably cotton fabric, approximately 50 in. (125 cm) square, and a staple gun. It's a good idea to use gingham, checked, or striped cotton for your top fabric, because blocking often requires you to pin out along straight lines, or create accurate corners, and using a base fabric that already has grid lines is a great help.

Lay the top fabric right side down, then lay the batting (wadding) centered on top. Now place the board centered on top of that. Pull the top fabric taut, and secure each corner to the board with a staple. Turn the board over and make sure that the lines or checks are straight before you continue, then staple the fabric to the underside of the board at 1 in. (2.5 cm) intervals so that it is all secured.

Your board is now ready to use, at a fraction of the cost of a ready-made one!

Joining pieces

After weaving in the yarn tails and blocking, all that remains to be done before your piece is complete is to sew it up. One of the simplest and fastest ways to join pieces together is by oversewing (also known as overstitching). It is not suitable for all joins because it is not as strong as some seams, but it is useful for joining smaller pieces. In later workshops you will be shown other ways to join your pieces of work that are appropriate to the project for that workshop, and become progressively more advanced.

Oversewing to join
This is one of the simplest methods of joining two pieces of knitting. It is normally worked with both pieces right sides together.

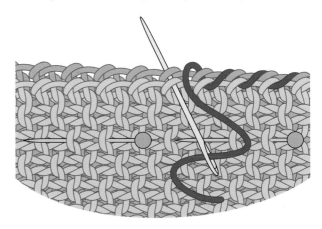

With both pieces right sides together and the edges to be joined aligned, take the yarn from the back of your work, over the edge of the seam and through the back again a short distance further on.

Rustic table runner

This table runner is made entirely with simple garter stitch squares. It will allow you to build your confidence in holding your yarn and needles, casting on, knitting, and binding (casting) off, and is a great portable project.

techniques used

Holding your yarn and needles

Cable cast on

Knit stitch

Binding (casting) off

Blocking and pressing

Oversewing to join

yarn

Sirdar Supersoft Aran (100% acrylic) worsted (Aran) yarn

3 x 3½ oz (100 g) balls—774 yd (708 m) —of shade 819 Peppermint

needles

Pair of US size 7 (4.5 mm) needles

other materials

Blunt darning needle

Ruler

Pins for blocking (preferably T-headed pins)

Steam iron and ironing board or blocking board

finished measurements

One square: 4½ in. (11.5 cm) square

Finished piece: 40½ x 13¼ in. (103 x 34 cm)

gauge (tension)

18 sts and 36 rows to 4 in. (10 cm) working garter stitch using US size 7 (4.5 mm) needles.

abbreviations

k	knit
rep	repeat
sts	stitch(es)
WS	wrong side

To make the square

(make 23)

Cast on 20 sts using the cable method.

Row 1: Knit to end.

Rows 2–36: Rep Row 1.

Bind (cast) off.

This forms one square module of the runner.

Finishing

Weave in the loose yarn tails (see page 25) using a blunt darning needle with a large eye, working the tails in and out of a few stitches along the row on the WS of the work. Trim off the tails.

Once you have made all the squares, block (see page 26) each of them to size and to an accurate square, as described. You will find that the corners have become very straight and the squares will be much neater and easier to sew together when they are all blocked. Repeat for all the other squares—you should be able to pin and steam four squares at a time, to speed things up.

Making up

Following the diagram of the completed runner, arrange two of the squares next to one another, so that one has the knitting running horizontally (square 1), and the other has the knitting running vertically (square 2). Place them right sides together and, using a length of yarn and a blunt darning needle, oversew the edges (see page 27). Weave in the loose tails. Join square 3 to square 2, so that all three squares sit in a line, using the same oversew method. You now have three squares in a line, running in horizontal/vertical/horizontal orientation. Join square 4 below square 1, with the knitting vertically. Join square 5 below square 3, again with the knitting in square 5 running vertically. Continue to build up the runner in this way, following the diagram for the orientation of the squares, until all 23 squares have been used. You should have four central holes within the piece.

Lightly press the completed piece.

Workshop 2

Knit and purl

Having mastered knit stitch, it is time to look at its companion, purl stitch. All knitting is constructed from a combination of knit and/or purl stitches, the most common version being stockinette (stocking) stitch. In this workshop you learn how to make a purl stitch and how to identify the knit and purl sides, and we will start to investigate the properties of knitted fabrics. The project to put all this into practice is an unusual Looped Necklace, made with the reverse side of stockinette (stocking) stitch as the right side.

Purl stitch

Purl is the other common stitch structure in knitting and when you have mastered it you will be able to create a range of different fabrics. Essentially, it is the same as a knit stitch, but worked from the reverse. So if you look at the reverse of a knit stitch you are looking at a purl stitch and vice versa (see page 32). Learning to work purl stitch means you can not only create stockinette (stocking) stitch, but also many other textured stitches such as ribbing and seed (moss) stitch—we look at these in subsequent workshops (see pages 36 and 44).

English method

Place the needle with the cast-on stitches in your left hand and the empty needle in your right. Thread your yarn around your right hand, as shown on page 15.

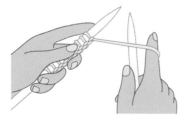

1 At the start of the first row, instead of placing the working yarn behind the tip of the left needle—as you would to begin a knit row—bring it to the front of both needle tips as shown here.

2 Insert the right needle into the front of the first stitch, from right to left. Wrap the yarn around the tip of the right needle, from right to left.

3 Pull the yarn through the stitch, to form a new stitch on the right needle.

4 Now slip the original stitch off the left needle by moving the right needle gently to the right. One purl stitch made.

Repeat steps 2–4 until you have worked all the stitches on the left needle. To continue, switch the needles over and start again with the full needle in your left hand.

Continental (German) method

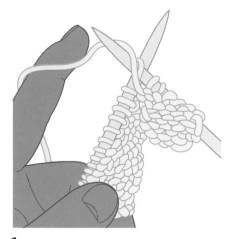

1 Place the needle containing all the stitches in your left hand and insert the tip of the right needle into the front of the first stitch, from right to left.

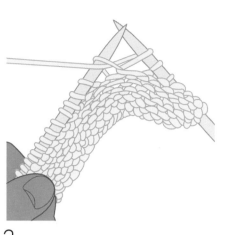

2 Hold the yarn at the back of the work, and keep it quite taut, but not tight. Pick up a loop of yarn with the tip of the right needle.

Using the curl

Because stockinette (stocking) stitch fabric involves knitting all the stitches on one side and purling all the stitches on the other, it has a natural curl. Rather than try and correct this, as is commonly the case (see The qualities of stockinette (stocking) stitch, page 32), you could choose to exploit this quality and create pretty rolled edges to your sweaters, necklines, or hats. In our next project, the Looped Necklace, we have made full use of this curl and it forms the main feature of the piece itself.

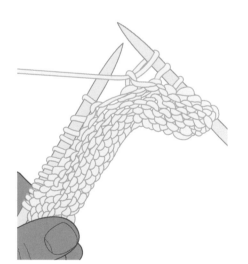

3 Use the tip of the right needle to draw this loop through the original stitch. This may feel trickier than making a knit stitch, but it is easy once you get used to the movements.

Slip the original stitch off the left needle by moving the right needle gently to the right. Repeat steps 1–3 until all the stitches on the left needle have been used up.

Stockinette (stocking) stitch

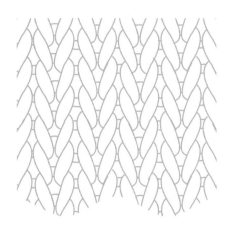 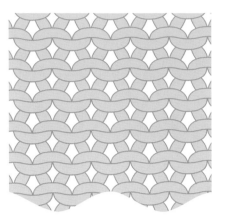 

Stockinette (stocking) stitch is the most common knit structure—once you can identify it, you will spot it everywhere: your T-shirts, your sweatshirts, even your socks!

To create stockinette (stocking) stitch you work a row knitting every stitch and then in the next row you purl every stitch. Alternating these two rows makes a fabric with one very smooth side of V stitches and one more textured side of horizontal bars. The former is the knit side, the latter the purl side. As we mentioned earlier, the back of the knit-stitch row makes a purl row on the purl side (above left), and the back of the purl-stitch row forms a knit row on the knit side (above center). Try and follow the path of the yarn along one row with your finger: you will see that it is doing the same thing, but you are seeing it from either side.

The qualities of stockinette (stocking) stitch

In Workshop 1 we saw that garter stitch (see page 24) lies flat and is a relatively robust fabric. However, stockinette (stocking) stitch has a natural curl at the edges, is somewhat stretchier than garter stitch, and works up comparatively narrower. These properties become important when you become competent enough to start adapting patterns or even designing your own. In order to make a piece of stockinette (stocking) stitch knitting lie flat it is usual to add a border or edge of garter stitch, seed (moss) stitch (see page 44), or ribbing (see page 36), or even a hem.

When working stockinette (stocking) stitch you are always knitting into the knit side of the fabric (the smooth side, with all the Vs) and you are always purling into the purl side (the side with all the little horizontal bars).

It is very important that you keep an even gauge (tension) because stockinette (stocking) stitch is a smooth, uniform, fabric and mistakes or changes in gauge (tension) will be very visible.

Stockinette (stocking) stitch is usually used with the knit side as the right side, and the purl side as the wrong side. Sometimes, however, the purl side is used as the right side—as in the Looped Necklace that follows—in which case it may be called reverse stockinette (stocking) stitch. This is most common in cable or bobble patterns, because it helps to highlight the textural effects.

Counting rows and stitches in stockinette (stocking) stitch fabric

It is far easier to count on the knit side of the fabric—each V (not upside-down V!) represents one stitch. To count rows in stockinette (stocking) stitch, follow a vertical line of Vs upward—each V represents one row.

To count stitches on the needle, pick along the needle with your finger, moving the stitches along and counting in twos for speed. To count the stitches in the fabric, follow one row of Vs along from one edge to the other.

Another joining method

Sometimes you need a seam that is more robust and more elastic than that provided by oversewing. In particular, the shoulder seams on sweaters or seams on heavier-duty items such as bags are generally worked in backstitch. This is because it can take more pulling, and therefore more weight

being placed on it, than many other types of seam. With this stitch you are always working back on yourself, hence the name "backstitch." You will see on the back that the stitches are much longer than those on the front and partly overlap each other—this is correct.

Backstitch to join

Backstitch is a commonly used method of joining pieces where the requirement is for a stable seam that is strong and less elastic than most other joining methods. It is worked in the same way as on woven cloth.

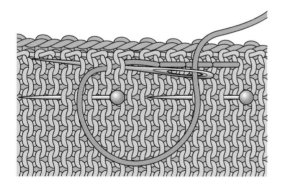

Place both pieces right sides together, with the edges to be joined aligned. Pin carefully along, approximately 1 in. (2.5 cm) in from the edge. Try to make sure the pieces line up with each other with stitches corresponding—this is particularly important when there is any kind of texture or colored pattern in the knitting. Thread a blunt darning needle with a length of the same yarn or, in the case of a colored pattern, use the main color or background color.

Insert the needle at the right-hand corner through both pieces of knitting and as close as you can get to the edge, from front to back. Bring the needle back through to the front one or two knitting stitches along in a straight line. Insert the needle back in the same space that

you started, from front to back, and bring it back through to the front so that it appears one or two knitting stitches along from the end of the last stitch. Insert the needle at the end of the last stitch worked, from front to back, and bring it back through to the front so that it appears one or two stitches along from the last stitch. Repeat this to the end of the seam and fasten off both yarn tails securely before cutting.

Looped necklace

This funky project is easy to make and very adaptable: you can make as many or few loops as you like, or use different colors. We made four loops in soft pastels but it would look equally good in strong graphic colors or toning autumnal shades. This project allows you to master stockinette (stocking) stitch, while the thick yarn lets you keep a close eye on stitches and gauge (tension).

techniques used

Cable cast on

Binding (casting) off

Knit stitch

Purl stitch

Backstitch to join

yarn

Lion Brand Baby's First (55% acrylic, 45% cotton) bulky (chunky) yarn

1 x 3½ oz (100 g) ball—120 yd (110 m) —each of shade 099 Pixie Dust, shade 146 Sea Sprite, shade 156 Beanstalk, and shade 100 Cotton Ball

needles

Pair US size 10½ (6.5 mm) needles

other materials

Blunt darning needle

finished measurements

Length of one finished loop before stretching: 25½ in. (64 cm)

gauge (tension)

11 sts and 16 rows to 4 in. (10 cm) working stockinette (stocking) stitch using US size 10½ (6.5 mm) needles.

abbreviations

k	knit
p	purl
rep	repeat
RS	right side
sts	stitch(es)
WS	wrong side

Aftercare

To wear, hold all the loops so that they align and there is one central hole, then place around your neck and use as a necklace or over your head and wear as a headband.

Wash by hand and dry flat—if you hang this when wet the loops will greatly lengthen due to the weight of the wet fabric.

To make the loop
(make 1 in each color, or as many as you like)
Cast on 70 sts.
Row 1 (WS): K to end.
Row 2 (RS): P to end.
Rows 3, 5, and 7: Rep Row 1.
Rows 4, 6, and 8: Rep Row 2.
Bind (cast) off.

Finishing
There is no need to block this project.
Weave in all loose tails (see Workshop 1, Weaving in yarn tails/ends, page 25).

Making up
Take one strip and place it with the two short edges aligned and RS (purl sides) together. Thread a short length of the same yarn into the darning needle and stitch a seam using backstitch (see page 33) to join. Darn in loose tails.

Take the next strip and align the short ends as before but —before stitching—thread one end of it through the loop previously made so that the two will be linked when you sew the second one into a loop. Repeat with the remaining strips, threading each through one of the other loops before you start sewing. Once the piece is all joined, stretch each loop horizontally so that the curl becomes more emphasized and the edges close up on each other.

Workshop 3

Ribbing and pattern repeats

Learning how to vary the stitches in a row is one of the most useful skills you can acquire. This workshop teaches you how to alternate knit and purl stitches in the same row, in a regular repeating pattern, to create ribbing or rib—and we cover several variations. The project, a beanie, offers you the chance to apply these skills to create a cute baby hat.

Different types of ribbing

The term ribbing is used to describe a particular type of fabric with a regular pattern of alternating knit and purl stitches that is repeated every row. In order to make stockinette (stocking) stitch lie flat it is necessary to add a border or edging of another stitch structure, such as ribbing. Ribbing lies flat and is very stretchy—if you look at any sweater or pair of socks it is likely that you will spot some ribbing at the edges and it's useful for edging scarves, throws, and all manner of items. Ribbing has characteristically vertical ridges, which are usually the same width across the whole piece. A very basic ribbing structure is known as 1 x 1 ribbing, which means knit one stitch then purl one stitch repeated along the row.

Recognizing different stitches

In stockinette (stocking) stitch in Workshop 2 (see page 32) we noted that you always knit the knit stitches, and purl the purl stitches. Look at your stockinette (stocking) stitch knitting, noting the difference in appearance between these two stitches. In ribbing you also knit the knit stitches and purl the purl stitches, so being able to tell which is which is really useful as you progress across the row.

Basic ribbing
Use a bulky (chunky) weight yarn to practice with, if you can. Using a pair of needles that are two sizes smaller than recommended on your yarn ball band (the reason for this is explained on page 37), cast on an even number of stitches, at least 30.

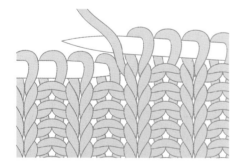

1 Place the needle containing all the stitches in your left hand. Tension the yarn as usual, and begin by holding it at the back of the work and working a knit stitch into the first stitch. Now, bring the yarn through the gap between the two needle tips, so that it sits at the front of the work.

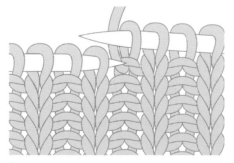

2 Work a purl stitch into the next stitch on the left needle. Then pass the yarn back through the gap between the two needle tips, to the back of the work, ready to work a knit stitch into the next stitch.

After working the knit stitch, bring the yarn through the middle to the front and work a purl stitch—you should now have worked four stitches. Repeat this pattern of moving the yarn to the back then the front, and working a knit then a purl stitch, until you have worked all the stitches. You may find moving the yarn back and forth a little laborious at first, but as you are able to hold the yarn more efficiently the process will speed up until it becomes second nature.

For the next row switch the needles so the full one is in your left hand. You finished the last row with a purl stitch, but now the reverse side is facing you so that last purl stitch will be worked as a knit stitch. So begin with a knit stitch and then alternate purl and knit across the row, again ending with a purl stitch. Work another 6 rows, then stop to examine the fabric you have produced.

The qualities of 1 x 1 ribbing

Ribbing fabric has a distinctive appearance, with vertical lines of knit stitches (Vs) that are raised up, next to indented troughs of purl stitches; if you look closely you will notice the horizontal bars of the individual stitches. This ribbing pattern looks the same on both sides of the fabric.

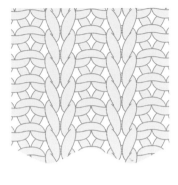

When working on an even number of stitches every row will be the same, because each one starts on a knit stitch and ends on a purl stitch, so the knit side of the last stitch is facing ready to start with a knit stitch on the next row. With an odd number of stitches you start and end one row with a knit stitch, and start and end the next row with a purl stitch. You still work in the same way, but alternating these two rows.

You will also notice that, despite casting on a reasonable number of stitches, the ribbing fabric seems a lot narrower—this is typical of ribbing. If you pull the fabric horizontally it will expand out to the size cast on. Let it go and it will spring back. This elasticity is the most useful characteristic of ribbing, and is why it is so widely used in knitted fashion. It allows for the creation of close-fitting items, stretchy fitted edges, and offers many shaping possibilities.

Additionally, ribbing is almost always worked in needles that are one or two sizes smaller than you would normally use. So, for example, if you are working in light worsted (DK) yarn and are making ribbing for the bottom of a sweater, you might use US size 3 (3.25 mm) needles for the ribbing sections, and (US size 6 (4 mm) needles for the stockinette (stocking) stitch main parts. This is because moving the yarn from back to front repeatedly between stitches when switching from knit to purl and vice versa adds to the stitch size and decreases the elasticity, so going down a needle size or two compensates for this and maintains the properties of the ribbing.

After looking at some other variations of ribbing we will take a look at binding (casting) off in ribbing (see page 38), which is a very useful skill to learn. It will allow you to maintain the stretchy quality of your ribbing when it occurs at the end of a garment.

Other common ribbing variations

You will encounter other variations of ribbing as your knitting skills increase. Some will have a completely regular pattern and will follow a similar formula; for example: knit two stitches, purl two stitches (written as k2, p2 and often known as 2 x 2 ribbing). This fabric looks the same on both sides.

Some will have a less regular pattern—for example, knit two stitches, purl one stitch (written as k2, p1 or 2 x 1 ribbing), or knit four stitches, purl two stitches (written as k4, p2). These more irregular patterns have a definite right (RS) and wrong side (WS) to the fabric, so take care to make sure you are working the RS pattern on the right side of your knitting, particularly if it occurs anywhere other than at the beginning of the work.

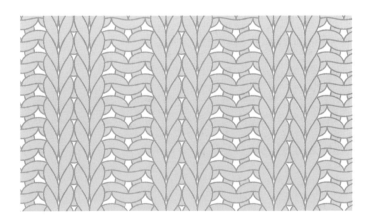

Working in ribbing

Like most other stitch patterns, it's important to keep track of stitch and row numbers as you work ribbing for a professional-looking result. Also, since ribbing by its nature is stretchy, it is better to bind (cast) off in ribbing to maintain the same elastic quality.

Counting rows and stitches in regular ribbing

As we have seen, when counting on the knit side of stockinette (stocking) stitch, one V equals one stitch and one row. Similarly in ribbing, you can count rows by counting the Vs in one vertical column.

To count stitches in ribbing, it can be helpful to count in repeats: for example, in 1 x 1 ribbing, you can count in twos if you count the columns of knit V stitches, but remember to adjust the total according to whether the edge stitches are knit or purl. In 2 x 2 ribbing, you can count in fours in the same way: you know that one ribbing column constitutes two knit stitches and that there are two purl stitches next to it, so every column represents a group of four stitches.

Binding (casting) off in ribbing

When you are working in a textural pattern it is good practice to bind (cast) off in the same way, maintaining the integrity of the pattern right up to the edge of the piece. To practice binding (casting) off in 1 x 1 ribbing, use the sample of basic ribbing you have just made.

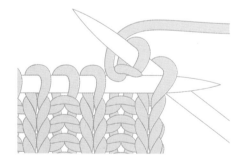

1 Place your needles as if you were about to start a new row. Knit the first stitch and purl the second one, as normal. Pass the yarn through to the back again, but do not knit the next stitch yet. Lift the first stitch over the last stitch on the right needle, and off the right needle, as for regular binding (casting) off. You will then have one stitch remaining on the right needle.

2 Repeat step 1, working the stitches on the left needle in ribbing, then binding (casting) them off as normal, until you have no more left on the left needle and only two on the right needle. Lift the first of these over the last, then cut the yarn and thread the loose tail through the remaining stitch to finish. Pull to close and weave in the loose end.

You should always aim to bind (cast) off in ribbing when you have just been knitting in ribbing, but follow the same pattern of ribbing you have been working, knitting the knit stitches and purling the purl stitches, then lifting the stitches over as for a regular bind (cast) off.

Other experiments to try out using ribbing

Try out a few different variations on ribbing and compare them to see how stretchy they are, whether the fabric looks the same on both sides, and how narrow they are compared to the same number of stitches worked in stockinette (stocking) stitch, garter stitch, or other ribbing variations. You may want to save the samples and your notes for future reference.

Slipping stitches

Sometimes it is necessary to move a stitch from one needle to the other without working a stitch into it—this is known as slipping a stitch and is a very simple technique. Although this is covered in much more detail in Workshop 7 (see page 68), you need to know how to work a basic slipped stitch to work the Fisherman's ribbing pattern on page 40, because the first stitch of every row is slipped rather than knitted.

Shaping with ribbing

Another experiment to try is using ribbing to add shaping in the middle of to an item. Cast on 20 sts and work 10 rows in stockinette (stocking) stitch, then 10 rows in 1 x 1 ribbing, then another 10 rows in stockinette (stocking) stitch. Note how the ribbed central panel is pulled in and shapes the rest of the piece. This is a neat way to add waist shaping when working garments, for instance.

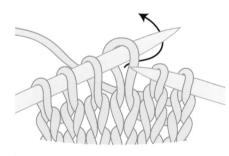

1 To slip a stitch knitwise, insert your right needle into the next stitch as if you were about to knit it, but instead of then wrapping the yarn, simply transfer the stitch off the left needle and onto the right one, without making a stitch. The yarn remains behind the work and is treated as normal for the following stitch.

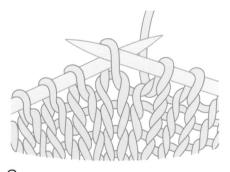

2 To slip a stitch purlwise, insert your right needle into the next stitch as if you were about to purl it, with the yarn at the front unless otherwise instructed. Instead of wrapping the yarn, simply transfer the stitch off the left needle and onto the right one, without making a stitch.

Knitting into the row below (k1b)

This is another technique you need for Fisherman's ribbing. Insert the needle into the center of the knit stitch immediately below the one you would normally work next—in other words, one row below. Complete the knit stitch as normal.

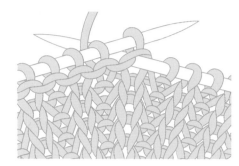

Fisherman's ribbing

This is a familiar-looking variation on ribbing, which appears thicker and more pronounced in texture. This effect is achieved by knitting into the row below, rather than the working row. Although this sounds complicated, it is very easy to achieve. This technique is also sometimes known as double stitch, and the resultant fabric is thick, soft, and grows very slowly. Always remember to slip the first stitch at the start of each row to avoid a wiggly, untidy edge.

Cast on an even number of stitches—for a practice swatch 30 stitches is a good number to work with.
Row 1: Purl every stitch to end (this is the foundation row).
Row 2: Slip first stitch (sl 1), [knit 1 below (k1b), purl 1 (p1)] to end.
Repeat row 2 for all subsequent rows.

Work until you have created a big enough piece to be able to look at the resultant fabric.

NB: If you had started with an odd number of stitches, you would need to adjust the pattern to accommodate this, as we saw with regular 1 x 1 rib (see The qualities of 1 x 1 ribbing, page 37).

Counting rows in Fisherman's ribbing

Counting rows in this stitch pattern is not as straightforward as counting rows in regular ribbing because you have worked into the row below. Each large V represents two rows in this instance, so bear this in mind for this pattern.

The project which follows, the Baby bobble hat, uses fisherman's ribbing, regular 1 x 1 ribbing, and plain stockinette (stocking) stitch and will demonstrate how ribbing offers both elasticity and a simple method of shaping knitted items.

Understanding pattern multiples

Knitting patterns employ square brackets when you need to repeat the same sequence of stitches many times. This concise system helps knitters stay on track in a pattern and simplifies the instructions.

For example, if you are working a row of knit one, purl one (k1, p1, or 1 x 1) ribbing, it would usually be written "[k1, p1] to end." This means you must repeat everything within the square brackets over and over again, in sequence, to the end of the row.

More complicated patterns use the same system. For instance, you may see something like: "K4, [p2, k4] 3 times, [p2, k10] twice, [p2, k4] 4 times." To work this sequence you knit the first four stitches, then work everything in the first set of brackets three times, then work everything in the second set of brackets twice, and finally work everything in the last set of brackets four times.

Note that square brackets are used to denote a repeated pattern sequence, while regular rounded brackets are used to show size variations in a pattern. Many knitting patterns offer a range of sizes, and instructions will differ slightly for each size for number of stitches, rows, or repeats.

As an example, the project in this workshop is written for three different sizes. If you are making the second size, for example, you should follow the second number given, which is the first one inside the brackets. So if the instructions are to cast on 60(**68**:80) sts, you cast on 68 stitches because 60 is the smallest size and 80 is the largest.

So on a pattern row for an item with multiple sizes you may see something like:
"K4, [p2, k4] 3(**4**:4) times, [p2, k10] 2(**3**:4) times, [p2, k4] 4(**5**:5) times.

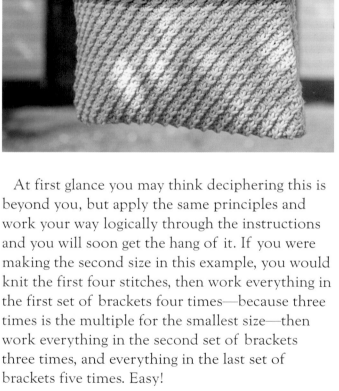

At first glance you may think deciphering this is beyond you, but apply the same principles and work your way logically through the instructions and you will soon get the hang of it. If you were making the second size in this example, you would knit the first four stitches, then work everything in the first set of brackets four times—because three times is the multiple for the smallest size—then work everything in the second set of brackets three times, and everything in the last set of brackets five times. Easy!

Baby bobble hat

This cute little hat has no shapings because the ribbing at the top draws the piece in naturally. The pompom was made with a plastic pompom maker, which greatly speeds up the process, but instructions are given for the card rings method. The hat can be made in three sizes, so use the guidance in the workshop to help you follow the size you need and to read the brackets.

techniques used

1 x 1 ribbing

Fisherman's ribbing

Stockinette (stocking) stitch

Binding (casting) off in ribbing

Reading pattern instructions and following a given size

Following multiples in pattern instructions

Oversewing and backstitch to join

Blocking

yarn

Rowan Baby Merino Silk DK (66% wool, 34% silk) light worsted (DK) yarn

1(1:2) x 1¾ oz (50 g) balls—147 yd (135 m) per ball—of shade 698 Jewel (A)

1 x 1¾ oz (50 g) ball—147 yd (135 m) —each of shade 670 Snowdrop (B), shade 675 Limone (C)

needles

Pair of US size 3 (3.25 mm) needles

Pair of US size 6 (4 mm) needles

other materials

Blunt darning needle

Pompom maker, larger size (optional)

size

To fit baby aged approximately 0-6(6–12:12–18) months

finished measurements

Circumference of hat at brim (unstretched)

15(17:19) in.

38(43:46) cm

gauge (tension)

20 sts and 30 rows to 4 in. (10 cm) working stockinette (stocking) stitch using US size 6 (4 mm) needles.

abbreviations

k	knit
k1b	knit one below
p	purl
rep	repeat
sl 1	slip one stitch
st(s)	stitch(es)
st st	stockinette (stocking) stitch
[]	repeat sequence within square brackets the number of times indicated

To make the hat
Using yarn A and US size 3 (3.25 mm) needles, cast on 79(89:99) sts.
Fisherman's ribbing section:
Row 1: P to end.
Row 2: Sl 1, [k1b, p1] to end of row.
Row 3: Sl 1, [p1, k1b] to last 2 sts, p1, k1.
Rep Rows 2 and 3 in sequence until you have worked a total of 16(20:24) rows in Fisherman's ribbing.
Change to US size 6 (4 mm) needles.
Stockinette (stocking) stitch section:
Row 1: K to end.
Row 2: P to end.

Rep last two rows until you have worked a total of 20(24:30) rows in stockinette (stocking) stitch.
1 x 1 ribbing section:
Row 1: K1, [p1, k1] to end.
Row 2: P1, [k1, p1] to end.
Rep this row until you have worked a total of 10(12:16) rows in 1 x 1 ribbing.
Bind (cast) off in ribbing (see page 38), leaving a long tail of at least 24 in. (60 cm).

Finishing
Block the piece (see Workshop 1, Blocking, page 26).

Making up

Thread up the yarn tail in the darning needle. Stitch in one stitch and out the next along the top edge of the hat. Draw the thread tightly closed, pulling as you stitch to close the top of the hat. Secure closed with a few further stitches, then secure the yarn tail on the inside of the top of the hat. The hat should now have a rounded top.

Pin the two right sides of the hat together along the back seam, and thread up a further length of yarn A in the darning needle. Insert the needle into the top of the back seam, as close as you can get to the drawn-in seam you just made. Oversew (see Workshop 1, page 27) the edge stitches of the 1 x 1 ribbing section, taking one stitch from each edge at a time. When you reach the stockinette (stocking) stitch section, backstitch (see Workshop 2, page 33) this part of the seam, working as close to the edge as you can. When you reach the Fisherman's ribbing section, oversew this part of the seam closed, taking the edge stitches into the seam.

Fasten off securely, and weave in the other loose yarn tail (see Workshop 1, Weaving in yarn tails, page 25) at the bottom of the work. The hat should now be beanie-shaped and is ready to wear if you do not want to add a pompom.

Pompom (optional)

Using either a pair of card rings cut to the size pompom you would like to create, or a pompom maker in the larger size, cut a length of yarn A and wind it around the rings until it runs out, then switch to yarn B and do the same, before then changing to yarn C and winding a further length. Repeat this sequence until the rings are completely full. Cut through the loops around the outer edge of the rings and ease them slightly apart. Thread a length of yarn between the layers and tie tightly, leaving a long end. Remove the card rings and fluff up the pompom. Use the long tail to stitch it in place very securely on the top of the hat. Trim off the yarn tail and any odd long ends.

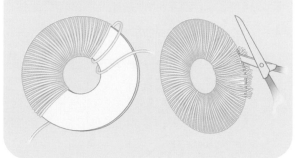

Workshop 4

Texture patterns

We have learned to combine knit and purl stitches to produce a textured fabric, but ribbing is just one of many texture patterns and in this workshop we look at some others. We also look at more complex instructions and learn how to correct some common mistakes. The Textured Pillow project gives you the chance to practice counting stitches as you work rows to create areas of different texture within a single row, which will also increase your skill in reading more complex knitting patterns.

Seed (moss) stitch

This is the simplest texture pattern, after ribbing (see page 36), and is worked in a very similar way. The difference is that in ribbing you knit every knit stitch and purl every purl stitch, but this pattern involves doing exactly the opposite. It is known as seed stitch in the USA and moss stitch in the UK.

Cast on an even number of stitches (30 is a good number for a test piece).
Row 1: [K1, P1] to end.
Row 2: [P1, K1] to end.
Work approximately 20 rows so that you can see what the fabric looks like. It should be textured with tiny raised loops. If you cast on an odd number of stitches, then every row would be as Row 1 above, ending with a K1.

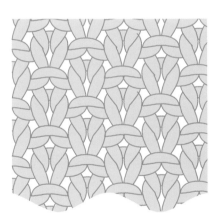

Larger seed (moss) stitch
A variation in number of repeats makes a similar textured but rather larger scale pattern.

Cast on 28 stitches this time (because you are working in multiples of 4 stitches).
Rows 1–2: [K2, P2] to end.
Rows 3–4: [P2, K2] to end.
By interspersing seed (moss) stitch with rows of plain knit, or purl, you can start to build up more complex gridded patterns. There are many variations on these types of texture pattern—the Textured Pillow in this workshop uses a "waffle" type pattern composed of simple knit and purl repeats. There are several excellent stitch directories with countless knitting stitch patterns if you would like to try out some more.

Brocades

This is the technical term for more involved patterns made by alternating knit and purl stitches to create texture and detail. Traditional fisherman's ganseys (also called guernseys) often feature this type of pattern—many of the designs have been passed down through generations, and are named for the fishing villages they came from. For example, there is a pattern known as "Polperro Laughing Boy," named after a tiny village in southeast Cornwall, a county in England.

For many such patterns you need to be able to follow a chart repeated at intervals, to avoid having detailed instructions written out each time. Above are some sample fabrics made in this way to whet your appetite, but we will return to working charts in more detail in Workshop 11, page 100.

Following more complex instructions

In Workshop 3 we learned how to apply a multiple bracketed instruction across a row of knitting (see page 41). For the project in this workshop you need to do this several times within a row because there are panels of different stitch patterns. This is a useful skill to learn because many of the more complex techniques, such as cables and lace, use this type of instruction. On a simpler level, you can create very effective patterns using only straightforward knit and purl.

Here is an example of a knitting pattern instruction that we will consider in more detail: "K2, [p4, k2] 4 times, p4, k6, [p4, k2] 4 times, p4, k6, [p4, k2] 5 times."

We already learned that square brackets denote something that must be repeated a given number of times. When instructions become longer and more complicated to follow, it is good practice to count your stitches from time to time as you work along the row, to make sure you have worked the right number of repeats.

So, in the example given you would first knit 2 stitches, then work the first set of bracketed instructions—[p4, k2]—four times. This should amount to a total of 26 stitches now worked: $2 + ([4 + 2] \times 4)$. Count the stitches on the right needle to make sure you have worked 26, then move on to the next set of instructions.

Work across the row, checking at intervals. This may be a little tedious but it will avoid having to rip out a whole row should you make a mistake—it is far easier to pick up a dropped stitch, or undo a few stitches, than to rip back many rows and lots of stitches. If you do make a mistake, the next few pages will help you sort out some common horrors.

Picking up a dropped stitch

However experienced you become, you will still drop a stitch from time to time. Spotted early it's easy to amend—but even if you don't see it for a few rows it's still relatively straightforward to put right. The best way to catch a dropped stitch early is to count your stitches often and regularly, and then you will see quickly if you have too many or too few. If you have too few stitches, look along your knitting for a loose loop sitting further back in your current row, or in the rows below—this is your dropped stitch. If you are not able to deal with it immediately, then insert a stitch holder into it to prevent it from dropping any lower.

Catching a dropped stitch in the current row
The best way to correct this is to carefully undo each stitch already worked on the row, one by one.

1 To undo stitches in a knit row, with right side facing insert the left needle into the stitch immediately below the one last worked. Push the stitch off the right needle and pull the yarn to free it. Repeat for each stitch until you reach the dropped loop. The principle is the same to undo stitches in a purl row, except that you work from the wrong side.

2 Pick up the dropped loop on the right needle and then the strand of yarn behind it from front to back. Insert the left needle into the dropped stitch from back to front and lift it over the strand, so that the strand becomes the new stitch. Make sure it is facing the right way and not twisted. Now work as normal to continue your row.

Correcting more than one stitch

The same technique of undoing stitches as shown above can be applied should you discover you have made a pattern or color mistake earlier on in your current row—simply carefully pull back each stitch, one at a time, making sure that each one is replaced on the needle without twisting it, until you reach the offending stitch. Pull that one back too, then re-work it correctly and continue your row.

Catching a dropped stitch in the row immediately below

This is a little different, but no more complex. Work the current row along to the point where the dropped stitch is sitting, so it would be the next stitch if it were actually on the needles.

On the knit side of the fabric

 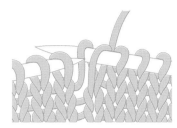  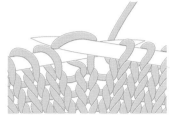

1 Make sure the horizontal strand of yarn between the correctly worked stitches is behind the stitch that has been dropped.

2 Insert the right needle into the dropped stitch loop, from front to back. Now poke the tip of the right needle from front to back under the strand of yarn behind the dropped stitch and lift this onto the right needle.

3 Keeping the working yarn tensioned fairly tightly in your right hand, use the tip of the left needle to lift the dropped stitch over the strand you just picked up, and off the right needle—like a binding (casting) off motion.

4 Use the tip of the left needle to transfer the stitch you have just repaired back onto the left needle, poking it in from front to back.

On the purl side of the fabric

This is worked in a similar way, with just a few differences.

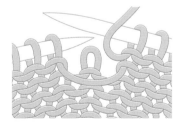 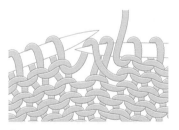 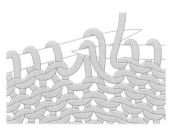 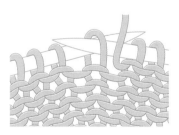

1 Make sure the horizontal strand of yarn between the correctly worked stitches is in front of the stitch that has been dropped.

2 Insert your right needle into the dropped stitch to catch it, but this time from back to front. Poke the tip of the right needle under the strand of yarn above the dropped stitch, from back to front this time, and lift it onto the right needle.

3 Keeping the working yarn tensioned fairly tightly in your right hand, use the tip of the left needle to lift the dropped stitch over the strand you just picked up, and off the right needle—like a binding (casting) off motion.

4 Use the tip of the left needle to transfer the stitch you have just repaired back onto the left needle, poking it in from front to back.

A magic way to correct knit/purl mistakes

This is slow, but if you notice that you have made a mistake in a knit and purl pattern (for example, you have worked a knit stitch where you should have purled) you can deliberately drop a stitch above where the mistake lies, then pull the stitch below out carefully until you reach the error. Now simply rework the stitches correctly using the crochet hook method as shown right, turning the work as needed.

Using a crochet hook to repair stitches dropped further down the work

Even if you spot your dropped stitch many rows after it has happened, do not despair; it is still possible to fix it, but you will need to tease out the adjacent stitches after you have worked it because both they and the repaired stitch are likely to be a little tight. This is because you are effectively creating an extra stitch from the yarn that has been used to make one row. If you know how to crochet, then the following will be an easy maneuver for you; if you don't, then you will understand the basic movement of crochet once you learn this technique.

For this type of repair, you will need a crochet hook that is slightly thinner than the needles you have been knitting with. These instructions show how to repair on the knit side of the work; to repair on the purl side, turn the work to the knit side and proceed in the same way.

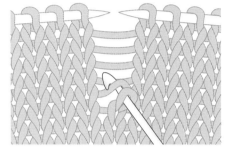

1 With right side facing, insert the crochet hook into the dropped stitch from front to back. Locate the next strand of yarn lying immediately above the dropped stitch and slide the crochet hook under it, then catch it with the hook. Twisting the hook so that it faces down, draw the strand of yarn through the dropped stitch that is already on the hook, thereby pushing the dropped stitch off. If you already understand crochet, this is effectively making a chain stitch.

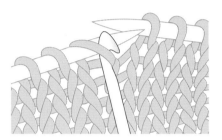

2 Continue in this way, taking the next strand of yarn above each time and working your way up the "ladder" until you have used the last loose strand. Transfer the last loop off the crochet hook and onto the left needle, making sure it is not twisted. Voilà! You have rescued your dropped stitch.

Repairing knitting with both knit and purl stitches

By using the technique above and employing a little patience, it is possible to repair a more complicated pattern. For example, if you noticed a dropped stitch in seed (moss) stitch you would need to repair a knit, then a purl, all the way up the ladder. Although this sounds as if it could be something of a nightmare, all you need to do is work with the crochet hook as follows: after working each strand, remove the hook from the stitch then turn the work to the other side so that a knit stitch is always what is needed, pick up the loop again with the hook and work the next strand as a knit stitch. Then turn again and repeat.

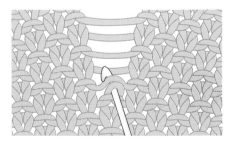

Correcting more than one row

If you spot a mistake that is further down the work and that involves more than one stitch, there may be no option but to rip back several rows. It is a little disheartening but always worth re-working the piece properly, rather than leaving a mistake and hoping it won't be noticed.

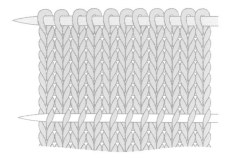

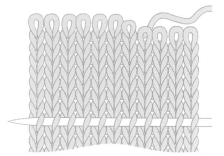

1 Find the row that lies immediately below the row containing the start of the mistake—so, effectively, the last row you worked that was completely correct. Take a knitting needle a couple of sizes smaller than the ones used for the work. Starting at the right-hand side, pass this thinner needle under the right-hand "leg" of each stitch along the entire row.

2 Remove the knitting needle at the top of your work (the one you have been knitting with) so that you expose all the stitches, then unravel them all, winding the yarn back up on the ball as you go along. Once you have unraveled down as far as the thinner knitting needle you should not be able to pull any further and you should have a needle full of stitches safely anchored.

If the working yarn is now sitting at the tip of the thinner needle then you are good to go—just work the stitches off this needle and onto your regular one, then discard the thinner needle and continue on your regular needles. If the working yarn is at the far end of the thinner needle you will need to carefully transfer the stitches, one at a time, onto one of your regular needles before continuing. Take care not to twist them as you

go. Then re-knit your pattern correctly on your regular needles from this point.

You should now be able to fix any mistakes that might crop up as you work your way through the remaining workshops and projects. The project that follows gives you a good opportunity to really get to grips with following pattern instructions, and working knit and purl stitches in a sequence to create a texture.

Checking the stitch count

Take great care to work along the SAME row—it is worth taking your time with this task. Make sure you have picked up each stitch; count the stitches on the thinner needle before going any further. If you have missed one, look carefully along the row to find the one you have missed, then pull the needle out to that point and pick it back up, then continue to the end of the row again.

Textured pillow

This is a soft cozy pillow with a textured panel design, designed by Pauline Richards. It is knitted in one piece and folded to create an envelope style opening, with a simple loop and button fastening.

techniques used

Cable cast on

Knit and purl texture patterns

Following a pattern and bracketed instructions

Creating different textures within a row

Backstitch to join

yarn

Debbie Bliss Cashmerino Aran (55% extra-fine merino wool/33% microfiber/12% cashmere) worsted (Aran) yarn

5 x 1¾ oz (50 g) balls—490 yd (450 m) —of shade 64 Cowslip or shade 47 Aqua

needles

One pair of US size 8 (5 mm) needles

One pair of US size 6 (4 mm) needles

other materials

Blunt tapestry needle

Button

16-in. (40-cm) square pillow form

finished measurements

Approximately 16 in. (40 cm) square

gauge (tension)

18 sts and 24 rows to 4 in. (10 cm) working stockinette (stocking) stitch using US size 8 (5 mm) needles.

abbreviations

foll	follows
k	knit
p	purl
patt	pattern
rep	repeat
RS	right side
st(s)	stitch(es)
WS	wrong side
[]	repeat sequence within square brackets the number of times indicated

To make the pillow cover

Using US size 8 (5 mm) needles, cast on 73 sts using the cable method.

Row 1: K to end.

Rows 2–8: Rep Row 1.

Work in patt as foll:

Row 1 (RS): K to end.

Row 2: P9, k9, p9, k19, p9, k9, p9.

Row 3: K9, p1, [k1, p1] 4 times, k9, p1, [k1, p1] 9 times, k9, p1, [k1, p1] 4 times, k9.

Row 4: P9, k1, [p1, k1] 4 times, p9, k1, [p1, k1] 9 times, p9, k1, [p1, k1] 4 times, p9.

Rep Rows 1–4 of patt until 88 rows of patt have been completed (for back).

Put a row marker at each end of last row—cut two small lengths of yarn in a contrast color and loop one through the first stitch and the other through the last stitch of last row.

Work 96 rows in patt (for front), putting row markers at each end of last row.

Work 37 rows in patt (for flap).

Next row: K to end.

Rep last row 6 times more

Bind (cast) off.

Finishing

Cover with a cloth or tea towel and press lightly on the WS. Weave in yarn tails (see page 25).

Making up

Using row markers as a guide, fold flap over with RS facing. Fold back section up over flap—the WS of back and front should now be on the outside.

Using backstitch (see Workshop 2, Backstitch to join, page 33) sew along both side edges of pillow cover, securing button flap between front and back layers.

Remove row markers and turn RS out.

Make button loop:

Using US size 6 (4 mm) needles, cast on 3 sts using cable method.

Next row: K1, p1, k1.

Rep this row 19 times.

Bind (cast) off, leaving a long tail to sew loop onto pillow.

Fold loop in half and sew each end to underside edge at center of flap. Take care not to stitch all the way through, so stitches won't show on outside of pillow.

Sew button in place to correspond with loop.

Insert pillow form and button up loop.

Aftercare

Remove the pillow form and hand wash or wash the
cover on a gentle wool cycle. Dry flat.

Workshop 5

Increasing stitches and looking at scale

In this workshop we look at a common and easy way of increasing the number of stitches on your needle, which will allow you to start creating interesting shapes. We also consider scale and how a simple project idea can be worked in different thicknesses of yarn to produce a diverse range of items. We discover that combining thinner yarns can create a thicker one, and we learn a more refined way to join seams. The project for this workshop, a selection of Curly Flower Pins, offers scope to put some of these ideas into practice.

Increasing

So far we have looked at making straight knitted pieces, but you will often need to widen or narrow your work as you go to make a more complicated shape. To widen your work you will need to increase the number of stitches on the needle at certain points in the work, and there are several different ways to do this. Here we cover bar increases, but more increasing methods and different ways to decrease stitches will be covered in the following workshop (see page 60).

Bar increase method (inc 1)
Now that you are confident in working knit and purl stitches, you should find the maneuvers involved in this technique to be straightforward. This is an increase and is abbreviated to "inc 1" in knitting patterns. You can purl into the front and back of a stitch in exactly the same way, though this can be a little fiddly to accomplish at first.

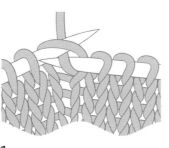

1 Knit into the stitch to be increased into as normal, but do not slip the old stitch off the left needle yet.

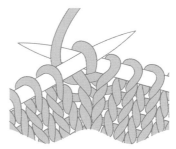

2 Knit into the back loop of the same stitch by inserting the needle from front to back, then lift it off the left needle.

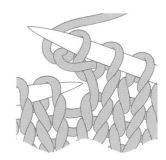

3 You should now have an extra stitch on the right needle. Continue knitting as normal.

Keeping the gauge (tension) correct

Try not to pull too tightly on the yarn as you work the increases, otherwise you will find them hard to work in the following row. To adjust the tightness if you need to, pull the right needle upward very slightly after each move and before slipping the stitches off the needles: this will take a little bit more yarn into the stitch, providing it with more flexibility.

Practicing increasing

To try out the bar increase method, work the following sample swatch.

Cast on at least 20 stitches, work a few rows in regular stockinette (stocking) stitch, then increase as follows:
Increase row (RS = knit side): K2, [inc 1, k1] to end.
Work 4 more rows of stockinette (stocking) stitch.

Multiple increases

It is also possible to increase twice in one stitch, thereby creating two new stitches, using the same basic method. This is a less common practice, but we will make use of it in the following project, the Curly Flower Pins.

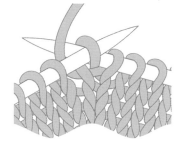

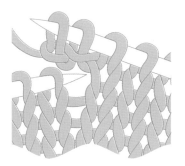

1 Repeat steps 1 and 2 of the inc 1 method opposite, but do not slip the stitch off the left needle after working into the back loop.

2 Knit once again into the front of the same stitch, before slipping it off the left needle. You should now have two extra stitches.

You will notice that both these increases create a little "bar" at their base, where the yarn was brought to the front, and this can be very helpful when trying to keep track of your increases. For example, if you are knitting a sleeve you may see instructions to "increase one stitch at each end of every 10th row." There should be one of these tell-tale little bars at the edge of every row in which you have increased, so you can count the rows in between to ensure you are increasing on the 10th row every time.

Make a practice piece and create some increases in knit and in purl as above, until you feel confident. The project that follows is a really quick piece that uses increases to create a spiral shape.

When increases are made in a garment they are rarely worked on the very edge stitch, because this can look very messy. Instead, increases and decreases are worked on the 2nd or 3rd stitch in from the edge, which creates a much neater finish and is known as "fully fashioned" shaping—we will return to this in Workshop 12, page 109.

Creating increases evenly throughout a row

Sometimes knitting pattern instructions may ask you to "increase X amount of stitches evenly throughout the next row"—it is particularly common in patterns with ribbing at the bottom of a front, back, or sleeve that then changes to stockinette (stocking) stitch. This set of increases opens out the rib and makes a much neater transition between the two types of knitted surface.

Where to increase is very simple to work out—you just need to make sure all your increases occur at even intervals in the row—but there are some things to take into consideration. If you have 64 stitches and you have to make eight increases, you might initially think that you should increase one stitch every eight stitches. However, that would leave you increasing in the very last stitch, which is not a very

neat solution. Much better to work the first four stitches then inc 1, then work [8 sts, inc 1] 7 times, before working the last 4 stitches.

In cases where there are a difficult number of stitches to increase—for example, six increases over 64 stitches—you have to use a little judgement. Use the method above, but add an extra stitch in at even intervals to accommodate those that do not fit neatly into the even distribution. In this example, it would be best to knit 12, inc 1, [k10, inc 1] 5 times, k12. You have maintained even increases—and because the extra four stitches are at the edges of the work, they will be partly incorporated into the seams.

There are other methods of increasing, some of which will be covered in later workshops. For methods of decreasing see Workshop 6, page 60.

Working with different gauges of yarn and needles and combining yarns

In general it is best to choose the recommended size of needles for the thickness of yarn you are using. The needle size will be given in the pattern instructions, but is also determined by the gauge (tension) required (see Getting started, Making a gauge (tension) swatch, page 18), which may mean adjusting the needle size to make sure that the finished piece will be the right size.

Sometimes, however, you may come across a project that you feel would look great worked in a completely different thickness of yarn and needles. Home decor pieces often fall into this category, as do some accessories. Consider how a fine-gauge delicate lace tablemat might look if it were scaled up and made with super-chunky yarn

and huge needles—you could create a fabulous floor rug without changing the pattern.

It is also possible to use two balls of yarn worked together, to form a thicker yarn. This takes practice, and you must be careful to make sure you always work with both strands at the same time, otherwise you will quickly gain stitches you did not intend. However, it gives lots of scope for combining colors and textures in interesting ways. Wind the yarns together into one ball before you start; this is because if one of the separate yarns should become snagged on something while you are working it will affect your gauge (tension) and make for untidy knitting. If they flow together this is far less likely to happen.

Rough equivalents

2 strands of sport (baby/3-ply) yarn is approximately equal to 1 strand of worsted (Aran) weight yarn:
US size 7 (4.5 mm) needles

2 strands of fingering (4-ply) yarn is approximately equivalent to 1 strand of light worsted (DK) yarn:
US size 6 (4 mm) needles

2 strands of light worsted (DK) yarn is approximately equivalent to 1 strand of chunky yarn:
US size 10½ (6.5–7 mm) needles

2 strands of worsted (Aran) yarn is approximately equivalent to 1 strand of bulky (super chunky) yarn:
US size 13–15 (9–10 mm) needles

You can also combine yarns of different weights; use the guide (see left) to help you work out what needle size to use. Experiment with the Curly Flower Pins project that follows—they are very small, so if you do not like the results, you have not wasted much time or yarn.

Feeling able to see other possibilities within pattern instructions is a liberating step for a new knitter. It is exciting to feel confident enough to choose between following patterns exactly or adapting them to your own ideas. The project on page 57 can be made out of any thickness of yarn and needles. Its end uses are up to you: there are several variations shown, so have fun with it and be brave in your experiments.

Joining seams with mattress stitch

Now that your knitting skills are becoming more advanced, it is time to learn a more professional method of joining seams to give a more refined finish to your pieces. This method is known as mattress stitch and it can be worked on horizontal or vertical seams. When used horizontally, it is sometimes called fake grafting.

You will need a piece of stockinette (stocking) stitch knitting to practice this seaming method—if possible use the one you made in Workshop 2 with no increases or decreases. If you no longer have it, knit up a piece of stockinette (stocking) stitch with at least 20 stitches and 20 rows. Make another one in the same size and gauge (tension).

Mattress stitch worked on vertical edges

The steps below cover how to work mattress stitch in stockinette (stocking) stitch, but can be applied to ribbing once you grasp the technique. Examine the piece with the knit side facing you and right side up. The knit side of stockinette (stocking) stitch resembles rows and columns of Vs; if you pull gently on one edge to reveal the gap between the edge stitch and the next one in, you will see a little horizontal bar between them. This is known as the running thread and you will be sewing in and out of it to create the seam.

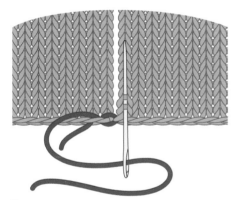

1 Hold the two pieces of knitting side by side, with right sides facing, and thread up a darning needle with a length of yarn (use a contrast color for this practice seam so that you can see it, but on a project use the same yarn as the main color). Starting at the bottom of the right-hand piece of knitting, insert your needle under the first two running threads and out again at the top of them.

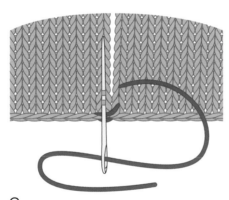

2 Now take the needle under the corresponding pair of running threads on the left-hand piece of knitting, and out at the top again in the same way.

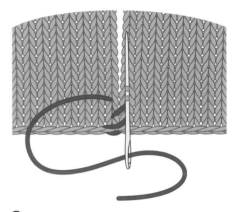

3 Insert the needle into the space where you ended the first mattress stitch on the right-hand piece of knitting, and work it under the next two running threads and out the top again.

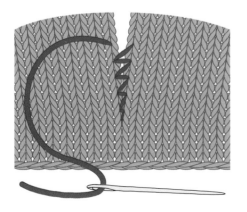

4 Insert the needle into the space where you ended the first mattress stitch on the left-hand piece of knitting, and work it under the next two running threads and out the top again. Repeat steps 3 and 4 along the entire seam, stopping every 10 or so stitches to pull the yarn firmly, but not too tightly, to join the two pieces together. Repeat until you have reached the top of the join, and fasten the yarn tails off securely.

You should have created a very neat join, which should be almost invisible. To work a similar join on a garter stitch or seed (moss) stitch piece, work a little closer to the edge to help the edges close more neatly, and take the purl "bars" instead of the running threads, otherwise work in the same way.

Multi-stranded roses with spirals

For the roses we have combined more than one strand of yarn to produce a thicker, multi-colored yarn. See page 54 for equivalent thicknesses when you combine yarns, and Getting Started page 10 for which needles to match with each thickness. The spirals are made from leftover scraps of light worsted (DK) yarn—try oddments of the silk used in the Beaded Clutch Purse (page 156) for a touch of luxury.

Multi-stranded roses

Make 3 roses following the instructions for the Chunky Curly Roses Pin, combining a different color with cream for each.
Spirals:
With a single yarn, make 3 curls following the instructions for Pink and White Twists, using a different color for each. Allow one of the curls to spiral in the same way as the roses, and secure with a few stitches.

Making up

Arrange the roses and spirals on an oval of felt and sew in place. Add a safety pin to the reverse, as for the Chunky Curly Roses Pin.

Pink and white twists

This pin uses the same technique but does not have the base knit row, so the curl is very defined and becomes a curlicue rather than a spiral disc. We have grouped several of these together for our pin; make as many as you wish and stitch them into a pleasing arrangement. This pin looks great as a method of fastening the Short-row Wrap (see page 77).

Using US size 6 (4 mm) needles and first yarn, cast on 25 sts.
Curl row: K into the front, back, then front again of every st. (75 sts)
Bind (cast) off.
Repeat for as many curls as you wish to make—we made 1 in Snowdrop and 7 in Candy .

Making up

Arrange the twists on a 2 in. (5 cm) felt circle. Stitch down and add the safety pin to the reverse, as for the Chunky Curly Roses Pin.

Other applications

Besides grouping the flowers together to make these pretty pins, they can be attached to other items such as ballerina pumps, purses, and the hems or collars of sweaters or shirts—use your imagination! As they are all made in one piece, they are also suitable to attach to baby or children's clothing or blankets.

Workshop 6

Decreasing and working color in stripes

In Workshop 5 we learned how to increase the number of working stitches; we now look at several ways to decrease stitches. These two skills will allow you to make pieces that are more complicated in shape. We also take a look at how to change color at the end of a row and the various effects that can be achieved in different texture patterns by adding stripes. The project in this workshop, a Man's Slouch Beanie, requires you to decrease in two ways, sew up with the new method learned in Workshop 5 (see page 55), and change color several times across different textures.

Shaping

The process of increasing or decreasing stitches to shape the knitting is often known as shaping and you might see this as a heading in knitting pattern instructions. It is separated out so that you know when to begin working the increases or decreases within the knitting. When you need to decrease (or, less commonly, increase), more than two stitches at a time at the edge of a piece, you bind (cast) off or cast on accordingly. This produces a very defined edge, however, so to achieve a more gradual slope you must increase or decrease by only one or two stitches at a time.

Decreasing and increasing for other purposes

Sometimes, increases and decreases are worked to provide texture or movement in the knitting, without necessarily changing the shape of the piece as a whole. In such cases the overall number of stitches is balanced out each time: logically, if you have decreased and now have one stitch fewer but you do not want the knitting to narrow in, then you must increase somewhere else in the row to ensure that this does not happen. The same is true in reverse. This is particularly apparent in the technique of lace knitting, which we will cover in Workshop 15 (see page 128).

Directional shaping

In Workshop 5 we used a simple method of increasing (see page 52) that creates a telltale bar at the base of the increased stitch, but does not affect the direction of the columns of stitches. When you are decreasing stitches the method you use will always determine whether, on the knit side of the fabric, the decrease looks neat and slants in the same direction as the edge of the work, or whether it goes against the direction and will be more noticeable. Decreases are harder to spot on the purl side, so issues of neatness

are of concern only when the knit side is to be the right side. For example, if you are knitting a sleeve you will need the work to narrow in toward the top of the sleeve at both sides. To make it look neat you will need to use a decrease method that slants to the left on one side and a different one that slants to the right on the other side, to match the slope of the sleeve as it narrows. The two methods shown below are commonly used in tandem in knitting pattern instructions where a symmetrical shape is required.

Knit 2 together (k2tog)

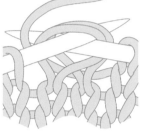

The most straightforward of all the decreases, this simply involves inserting the right needle into two stitches rather than one, from front to back, and knitting as though they were one stitch. The top loop of the resulting stitch leans slightly toward the right, and therefore this technique should be used at the left-hand edge of the shaping, to create a slope inward from left to right.

Purl 2 together (p2tog)

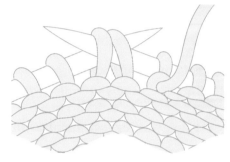

You can also purl two stitches together in the same way: insert the right needle into two stitches instead of one, and purl them as if they were one stitch. This stitch also leans toward the right, creating a slope inward from left to right.

Slip 1, knit 1, pass slipped stitch over (sl 1, k1, psso)

To work a decrease that slants toward the left, and which can be used at the right-hand edge of the shaping, you need to use a different technique.

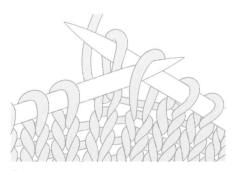

1 Slip one stitch knitwise so that you have a stitch on the right needle that is not knitted, but slipped. See page 39 for how to slip stitches knitwise if you have forgotten.

2 Knit the next stitch on the left-hand needle as normal.

3 Insert the tip of the left needle across the front of the slipped stitch, from left to right, as shown, and lift it over the knit stitch and off the right needle, as if you had bound (cast) it off. You will notice that the resulting decreased stitch leans to the left, creating a slope inward from right to left.

Man's slouch beanie

A generous casual slouch hat that has a subtle knit and purl texture pattern coupled with a varied stripe effect, this project will give you the chance to practice your decreases and to see how they can be used to create an unexpectedly 3-D shape from a flat piece of knitting.

techniques used

Knit and purl texture patterns

Rib

Changing color

Decreasing by k2tog, p2tog, and ssk

yarn

Cascade 220 Superwash wool, (100% wool) light worsted (DK) yarn

1 x 3½ oz (100 g) ball—218 yd (200 m) —each of shades 904 Colonial Blue Heather (A), 1910 Summer Sky Heather (B), 892 Space Needle (C), 1914 Alaska Sky (D)

needles

Pair of US size 6 (4 mm) needles

other materials

Blunt darning needle

finished measurements

Circumference around crown: 20½ in. (52 cm)

gauge (tension)

20 sts and 26 rows to 4 in. (10 cm) working stockinette (stocking) stitch using US size 6 (4 mm) needles.

abbreviations

cont	continue
dec	decrease
k	knit
k2tog	knit 2 stitches together
p	purl
p2tog	purl 2 stitches together
patt	pattern
rep	repeat
ssk	slip, slip, knit 2 stitches together
st(s)	stitch(es)
[]	repeat sequence within square brackets the number of times indicated

To make the beanie

Using yarn A, cast on 104 sts.

Row 1: Rib patt [k2, p2] to end.

Work 7 more rows in rib patt as set by Row 1. 8 rows

Change to yarn B, work 4 rows in rib patt (12 rows).

Change to yarn A, work 2 rows in rib patt (14 rows).

Change to yarn B, work 2 rows in rib patt (16 rows).

Change to yarn C, work 2 rows in rib patt (18 rows).

Change to yarn D, work 2 rows in rib patt (20 rows).

Change to yarn C, work 2 rows in rib patt (22 rows).

Next row: K to end.

Next row: P to end.

Begin texture patt section:

Using yarn C, work 8 rows of texture patt:

Texture row 1: K1, *p1, k5; rep from * to last st, k1.

Texture row 2: P1, *k1, p3, k1, p1; rep from * to last st, p1.

Texture row 3: K1, *p1, k1; rep from * to last st, k1.

Texture row 4: P1, * k1, p1; rep from * to last st, p1.

Texture row 5: K1, *k2, p1, k1, p1, k1; rep from * to last st, k1.

Texture row 6: P1, *p2, k1, p3; rep from * to last st, p1.

Texture row 7: K to end.

Texture row 8: P to end.

This 8-row sequence forms texture patt.

Rep texture patt sequence using yarns as follows:

2 rows in yarn A.

2 rows in yarn D.

4 rows in yarn A.

6 rows in yarn B.

2 rows in yarn C.

Change to yarn B.

Next row (dec row): K4, [ssk, k1, k2tog, k8] to last 9 sts, ssk, k1, k2tog, k4. 88 sts

Next row: P to end.

Change to yarn C.

Next row: P to end.

Next row: P to end.

Next row: K to end.

Next row: P to end.

Cont in texture patt.

6 rows in yarn D.

2 rows in yarn C.

6 rows in yarn A.

8 rows in yarn B.

Change to yarn C.

Next row: K to end.

Next row (dec row): K3, [ssk, k1, k2tog, k6] to last 8 sts, ssk, k1, k2tog, p3. 72 sts

Next row: P to end.

Next row: K to end.

Change to yarn D.

Next row: K to end.

Cont in texture patt, beg at Row 1.

3 rows in yarn D.

3 rows in yarn C.

Shape top of hat:

Cont in st st only.

Next row: P to end.

Next row (dec row): K2, [ssk, k1, k2tog, k4] to last 7 sts, ssk, k1, k2tog, k2. 56 sts

Next row: P to end.

Change to yarn A.

Next row (dec row): K3, *k2tog, k5; rep from * to last 4 sts, k2tog, k2. 48 sts

Next row: P to end.

Next row (dec row): K2, *k2tog, k4; rep from * to last 4 sts, k2tog, k2. 40 sts

Next row: P to end.

Next row (dec row): K1, *k2tog, k3; rep from * to last 4 sts, k2tog, k2. 32 sts

Next row: P to end.

Next row (dec row): K1, *k2tog, k2; rep from * to last 3 sts, k2tog, k1. 24 sts

Next row: *P2tog, p1; rep from * to end.

Cut yarn, leaving a long tail of yarn but do not bind (cast) off.

Finishing

Thread yarn tail into the darning needle and pass it through all stitches on the needle before letting each fall off the

needle. Draw up tightly closed so that the hat forms a circle at the top. Stitch closed securely, then fasten off. Weave in all loose yarn tails.

Making up

Using a length of yarn A, and starting at the bottom, sew the seam of the hat using mattress stitch (see Workshop 5, page 55). Take care to retain the rounded shape at the top part of the hat; the upper reverse stockinette (stocking) stitch ridge should form a "turn" that marks where the crown begins.

Fasten off at the top and weave in both yarn tails. Press lightly under a damp dish towel.

Workshop 7

Slip stitch patterns

In this short workshop we look at how to make a variety of slipped stitch patterns. In Workshop 3 we learned how to slip a stitch without knitting it (see page 39), but besides being a useful maneuver in its own right, this stitch offers a wealth of potential for textural and multi-color patterns. By combining slipped stitches with knit and/or purl, intricate patterns can be created—there are many of these, so if you enjoy this technique then see the suggested reading on page 171 for more ideas. The project is a fashionable Skinny Tie with a slip stitch pattern that is quick to work and makes a stylish gift.

The formation of slip stitch patterns

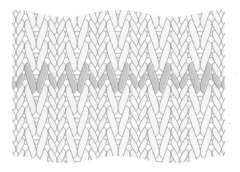

When you slip a stitch, the length of it increases to accommodate all the rows it occupies—the one(s) where it is slipped, and the one after where it is worked—so this elongated stitch is one aspect of the decorative nature of slipped stitches.

Slipping individual stitches creates a firm and stable fabric. Slipping more than one stitch in sequence produces a more dramatic effect, but at the expense of practicality—the longer the slipped "bars," the more prone to snagging they are, although in finer yarns this is less of an issue. Slipping stitches for one row at a time, then knitting or purling them in between, again creates a stable fabric. Slipping for more than one row at a time will produce puckering, which can be very effective in a regular pattern. If this is not what is intended, it may be counteracted by wrapping the yarn around the needles an extra time when it is eventually knitted, thereby elongating the stitch.

At the same time, when a stitch is slipped, the working thread has to travel from the stitch before it to the next stitch that is actually worked. This traveling thread forms little bars, which contribute to the textural nature of slipped stitch patterns.

Even more pronounced effects are produced by strategic alternating of colors: although you only use one color to a row in slipped stitch, the patterns achieved give the effect that you have knitted two colors in each row, and offer the opportunity for optical or subtle mixes of color.

Using slipped stitch techniques in patterns that also mix knit and purl extends the potential even further. We will practice a few types of slipped stitch pattern in this workshop, and compare the resultant fabrics to others we have made in terms of elasticity, length, width, and thickness.

Textural pattern

For this practice piece try to use a similar yarn and needle size to those you have used in other, earlier practice pieces. This will help you to compare the properties of the fabric you produce to your earlier practice pieces.

Cast on 30 sts.
Row 1: K to end.
Row 2: *K1, sl 1; rep from * to last 2 sts, k2.
Row 3: As Row 1.
Row 4: As Row 2.
Row 5: As Row 1.
Row 6: K2, *sl 1, k1; rep from * to end.
Row 7: As Row 1.
Row 8: As Row 6.
Repeat these 8 rows in sequence until you have worked another 3 sequences.

Note that in this example the texture mostly appears on the purl side of the fabric, because it is the little slip stitch bars that are creating the effect. Did you feel as if the fabric was growing rather slowly? It is a very subtle pattern because we are slipping only one stitch, and one row at a time, and have used only one color.

Two-color slip stitch pattern

Slip stitch patterns worked with more than one color are also sometimes called mosaic knitting. They tend to be geometric in pattern and often quite small scale. Checks, stripes, and gridded effects are easy to produce using this technique and the resultant fabrics lend themselves to thicker winter knits. Choose a second, contrast color that will be easy to see when worked with the one you are already using.

Continuing with the sample piece already begun, knit 6 rows of stockinette (stocking) stitch before starting this next sample pattern.
Row 1: Using your main color (yarn A), k to end.
Row 2: Still using A, p to end.
Row 3: Join in yarn B, k1, sl 1, *k2, sl 1; rep from * to last st, k1.
Row 4: Still using B, p1, sl 1, *p2, sl 1; rep from * to last st, p1.
Rep these 4 rows in sequence another 3 times. You should have a gridded pattern looking as if two colors have been worked within a row. The slipped stitches extend to cover the plain rows.
You could work Rows 1 and 2 in a different color each time for a more complex effect, but you would still never need to use more than one yarn at a time per row.

Managing colors

In Workshop 6 we learned how to join in a new color (see page 64). For this sample we carry the yarn not in use up the side of the work, so when you change color simply drop the yarn you are no longer using and pick up the other yarn. Slightly tighten the first stitch to compensate for any looseness that might occur, and manage the two yarn balls so they do not become twisted together as you work. Untwist them at intervals if you find this is happening.

Texture and color combined

The two previous samples used a stockinette (stocking) stitch basis for their construction—knit stitches on one side and purl on the other. Once you start to mix up the knit and purl stitches a little, and add some color changes in, far more complex-looking fabrics can be created. Our third sample will combine all of these elements.

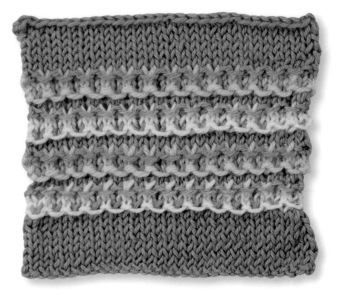

Choose two more contrast colors (C) and (D), to use alongside the existing two. Knit 6 more rows in stockinette (stocking) stitch in yarn A, to separate out the sample pieces again. On the last row, decrease one stitch by p2tog at the start of the row. This is to accommodate the sequence of stitches in this particular pattern.

Row 1: Using A, k to end.
Row 2: Still using A, p to end.
Row 3: Change to B, k1, *sl 1, k1; rep from * to end.
Row 4: Still using B, rep Row 3.
Row 5: Still using B, k to end.
Row 6: Still using B, p to end.
Row 7: Change to C, k2, sl 1, *k1, sl 1; rep from * to last 2 sts, k2.
Row 8: Still using C, p1, k1, *sl 1, k1; rep from * to last st, p1.
Row 9: Still using C, k to end.

Row 10: Still using C, p to end.
Row 11: Change to D, k1, *sl 1, k1; rep from * to end.
Row 12: Still using D, rep Row 11.
Row 13: Still using D, k to end.
Row 14: Still using D, p to end.
Row 15: Change to A, k2, sl 1, *k1, sl 1; rep from * to last 2 sts, k2.
Row 16: Still using A, p1, k1, *sl 1, k1; rep from * to last st, p1.
Repeat these 16 rows in sequence one more time.

Note how the addition of working in a sequence of stitches other than stockinette (stocking) stitch has created purl ridges, and the fabric has a complex appearance yet was simple to produce.

Properties of slip stitch fabrics

You will, by now, have noted that fabrics made of slip stitch patterns are slower to make. However, because you do not have to cope with multiple balls of yarn in one row, there are some compensations. Some other things to bear in mind about slip stitch fabrics are:

- They are sometimes narrower and shorter than most other knit fabrics.
- They tend to be thicker than other knit fabrics.
- They may curl rather more than other knit fabrics, unless there is a balance of knit and purl stitches within the structure.

Skinny tie

This quick project is a long slender piece of slip stitch, seed (moss) stitch and stockinette (stocking) stitch patterned knitting, with no shaping. It requires thorough blocking to help it lie flat, but the pattern is regular and easy to grasp.

techniques used

Knit and purl

Slip stitch

Changing color

Casting on and binding (casting) off

Yarn

Rowan wool cotton DK, (50% cotton, 50% merino wool) light worsted (DK) yarn

1 x 1¾ oz (50 g) ball – 123 yd (113 m) – each of shades 968 Cypress (A), 900 Antique (B)

Needles

Pair of US size 3 (3.25 mm) needles

Other materials

Blunt darning needle

Steam iron and ironing board

Pressing cloth or dish towel

Finished measurements

Width: 2 in. (5 cm)

Length: 52 in. (130 cm)

Gauge (tension)

24 sts and 48 rows (one repeat) to 4½ in. (11.5 cm) working main patt using US size 3 (3.25 mm) needles.

Abbreviations

beg	beginning
cont	continue
g st	garter st
k	knit
LH	left-hand
p	purl
patt	pattern
rep	repeat
sl	slip
st(s)	stitch(es)

To make the tie

Using yarn A, cast on 12 sts.

Rows 1–3: K to end.

Row 4: [K1, p1] to last 2 sts, k2.

Row 5: K2, [p1, k1] to end.

Rows 6–7: Rep Rows 4–5.

Row 8: Rep Row 4.

Beg main patt:

Row 1 (RS): K to end.

Row 2: K1, p10, k1.

Rows 3–4: Rep Rows 1–2.

Drop yarn B, do not break yarn A.

Row 5: Using yarn B, [sl next 2 sts purlwise, k1] 3 times, turn leaving 3 sts unworked on LH needle.

Row 6: Using yarn B, [k1, bring yarn between needles to WS, sl next 2 sts purlwise] 3 times.

Rows 7–8: Using yarn A, rep Rows 1–2.

Row 9: Using yarn B, sl next 3 sts purlwise, [k1, sl next 2 sts purlwise] twice, k1, turn leaving 2 sts unworked on LH needle.

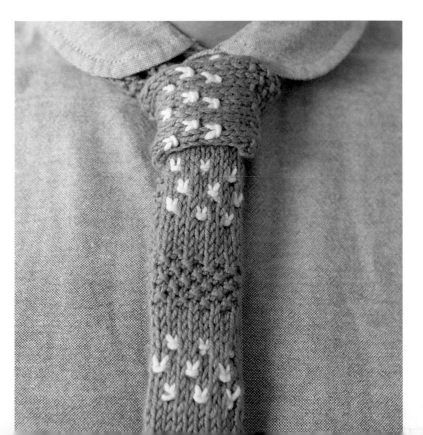

Row 10: Using yarn B, [k1, bring yarn between needles to WS, sl next 2 sts purlwise] twice, k1, bring yarn between needles to WS, sl last 3 sts.
Rows 11–12: Rep Rows 7–8.
Rows 13–14: Rep Rows 5–6.
Fasten off yarn B, cont in yarn A.
Rows 15–18: Rep Rows 1–4.
Row 19: K2, [p1, k1] to end.
Row 20: [K1, p1] to end.
Rows 21–24: Rep Rows 19 and 20 twice more.
Rows 25–28: Rep Rows 1–4.
Join in yarn B, do not break yarn A.
Rows 29–34: Rep Rows 9–14.
Rows 35–38: Rep Rows 7–10.
Fasten off yarn B.
Rows 39–48: Rep Rows 15–24.
These 48 rows form main patt.
Work the 48-row sequence a further 6 times, then work Rows 1–24 again.

*Cont in yarn A only.
Next row: K to end.
Next row: K1, p10, k1.
Rep last 2 rows once more.
Next row: K2, [p1, k1] to end.
Next row: [K1, p1] to last 2 sts, k2.
Rep last 2 rows twice more. *
Rep from * to * 12 times more.
Work 2 rows in g st.
Bind (cast) off.

Finishing
Weave in all loose yarn tails.
   Slip stitch is very prone to curling, so the tie will need firm blocking (see page 26). Pin flat in sections onto an ironing board, right side down. Place a damp cloth over the top and press with a steam iron set to the right temperature for the yarn used. Work along the tie, pinning it flat, until you have flattened out the whole thing. Roll up to store.

Workshop 8

Short rowing

Now that we have covered techniques in increasing and decreasing, you should be able to create many types of shaped pieces. However, there is another way to create interesting and unusual shapes and creative effects within your fabrics: short rowing, which involves turning the knitting before you get to the end of a row. This workshop also covers different yarn-over techniques and how they are used. The project, a pretty Short-row Wrap, is a more involved piece than we have made so far—but it is a regular repeat of the same panel and will build your skills in short rowing and making yarn overs.

All about short rowing

Normally you work along each row from the first stitch to the last stitch—but you do not have to do so. You can turn and work back again at any point in the row and this will make a shorter row within the piece—hence the term "short rowing." If you do this over and over again, turning at specific points, you can create a variety of effects and shapes, from triangles and circles to ruffles and ruching. It is also an essential technique for socks, because this is how the heel and toe are "turned."

There is really nothing particularly complex to know about this technique except that you should usually take care to avoid making holes as you turn the work. This is prone to occur because you will have made an extra little "edge" at each turn, so this tiny vertical edge creates a tiny hole in the row that can be unsightly. There may be times when you might prefer to leave these holes visible, but this is likely to be quite a rare occurrence.

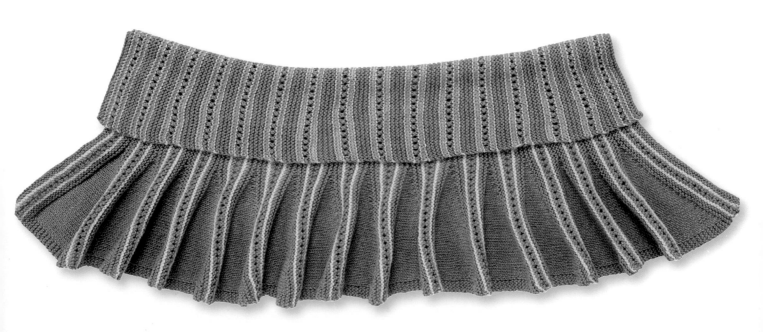

Properties of short rowing

Short rowing can be used to create flat circular or triangular shapes.

If it is worked in combination with a flat areas of knitting it can also be used to create a ruffle, as we have done in the project in this workshop.

The technique is also ideal to create three-dimensional shapes, such as the toe and heel of socks.

Avoid making holes when turning by making sure that you wrap the stitches at the end of each short row, whether they are knit or purl. The little wrap ties the short row to the unworked stitch next to it, sealing any potential hole.

Alternatively you could make the holes into a decorative feature.

Working short rows in the center

Short rowing will work in any stitch pattern, but the more complex the pattern, the harder it can be to match up the stitches at the end of a short-rowed panel, so this sample is worked in stockinette (stocking) stitch. As mentioned, you can decide to stop and turn the work at any point in the row. To begin with, we will work a central panel of short rowing.

Cast on about 40 stitches and work 10 rows in stockinette (stocking) stitch.
Next row: Knit 25 stitches. *Bring the yarn to the front (see Workshop3, Basic ribbing, step 1, page 36), and then slip the next stitch purlwise onto the right needle. Now pass the yarn to the back of the work again and slip the slipped stitch back onto the left needle. This is known as wrapping the stitch. Turn the work.
Next row: Purl 10 stitches. Pass the yarn to the back of the work, then slip the next stitch purlwise, before then bringing the yarn back through to the front again. Slip the slipped stitch back onto the left needle, and turn the work.

Knit 10 stitches and repeat from * one more time. You have created four short rows.
Next row: Knit all stitches to the end of the row. Turn the work and purl all the stitches to the end of the row.
Repeat the sequence about five more times. You will see that a gathered panel has started to develop in the center of the piece. A variation of this technique is used to turn the heels and toes of socks.

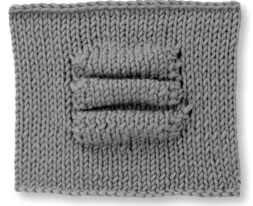

Working short rows at the edge

We will now look at the effect of working short rows at the edge of pieces, rather than in the center. To prepare, work a further 6 rows on your sample, working all the stitches of the row each time.

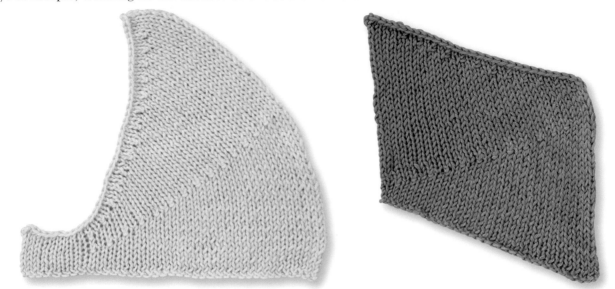

Next row: Knit 30 stitches, *bring the yarn to the front of the work, then slip the next stitch purlwise onto the right needle. Pass the yarn to the back again and slip the slipped stitch back onto the left needle. Turn the work**.
Next row: Slip the next stitch purlwise, then purl the last 29 stitches.
Knit 28 stitches, then repeat from * to **.
Slip the next stitch purlwise, then purl the last 27 stitches.
Continue in this way, working one stitch less each row as directed, until you only have 4

stitches left and you are about to work a purl row. Purl these 4 stitches as usual.
Knit 4 stitches, *lift the wrap thread in front of the next stitch back onto the left needle and knit together with the next stitch. Knit 1 stitch; repeat from * to end of row.
You should now have created a triangular panel. From this point, you can go on to make another triangle running in the same direction by purling all stitches on the next row then repeating the sequence again. If you make several of these in succession you will

eventually create a circular shape. The project in this workshop exploits this technique to create a curved wrap. Alternatively, you can work one more row of all stitches, leaving you with a purl row facing you next. If you then work the sequence again, but replacing all the knit instructions with purl and vice versa, you will have created a triangle that runs in the opposite direction. This technique is particularly effective when each direction is worked in a different color of yarn.

Working short rows to create a corner

It is also possible to create a sharp corner using short rowing. Instead of beginning the second panel with a long row, build up again from the shortest row, working one more stitch each row until you have in incorporated all the stitches again and have a full row.

Now that you feel confident to turn your work at various intervals in the row, you will also be able to tackle things like pockets, fingers of gloves, and necklines. These latter details do not use short rowing as a decorative feature, but do employ the skill of turning work within a working row.

Different types of yarn over

We learned some useful methods of increasing stitches in Workshop 5 (see page 52). There is another, very simple method of adding a stitch that is often done accidentally by new knitters: making a yarn over. Avoid using the yarn over as your chosen method of increase unless you are specifically instructed to do so; other methods we have already covered are much neater. However, it is often employed to create a decorative hole or eyelet and forms a fundamental part of the techniques involved in lace knitting.

There are also similar terms that can be rather confusing: yarn forward (yf or yfwd) refers to the same technique when making a yarn over on a knit row, while yarn round needle (yrn) applies to instances where the yarn is physically wrapped around the needle to create the new stitch. Although this may all sound very baffling, as you work the practice examples all will become clear. Once again, make a piece of stockinette (stocking) stitch to practice with, maybe 30 sts and 10 rows as a foundation, ending on a purl row.

Yarn over on a knit row (yf or yfwd)

Knit 4 sts. Bring the yarn to the front between the needles, then insert the right needle into the next stitch and knit as normal. As you carry the yarn to knit the stitch it makes an extra strand on the needle, which you treat as a regular stitch on the next row. Repeat a few times across the row.

Work 2 rows in stockinette (stocking) stitch. The row of yarn overs just made should look like a row of decorative holes.

Yarn over on a purl row (yo)

Purl 4 stitches. Take the yarn to the back of the work over the needle, then purl the stitch as normal. The extra strand created makes another stitch, which you should treat as normal on subsequent rows. Repeat another few times until you have grasped the technique clearly. End with a purl row, so you can practice the next move on a knit row.

Yarn round needle (yrn)

Sometimes you need to make a yarn over in a pattern combining knit and purl stitches, such as ribbing or seed (moss) stitch. Simply bringing the yarn to the front or back will not achieve an extra stitch, because this move is part of the pattern, so you need to wrap the yarn fully around the needle. Bring the yarn forward all the way round the needle, ending at the front again; or, take to the back, wrap all the way round, ending at the back again. End with a purl row.

Use yarn overs decoratively

The pretty effect of this simple technique is often used to make eyelet patterns. However, since each yarn over makes an extra stitch, if you want to maintain the same number of stitches within the row you must decrease a stitch to compensate for each one increased. The simplest way to achieve this is to k2tog immediately before or after working the yarn over, so that you are increasing and decreasing a stitch at the same time.

Practice the following sequence of rows a few times so that you can confidently work it in the wrap project that follows.

Row 1: K1, [yf, k2tog] to last st, k1.
Row 2: P all sts.

You now have a neat row of eyelets—and you also just learned the basic principle of lace knitting, which is covered in more detail in Workshop 15.

Short-row wrap

This is a larger project that takes a little longer to make, but which has a regular repeating pattern that is easy to pick up once you have knitted one or two panels. The instructions here will make a capelet shape, which can be secured at the neckline with a clasp or pin; if you would like to make a longer wrap that will extend over the shoulder again, then simply make more panels until you have your desired length.

techniques used

Yarn over

Knit 2 together

Short rowing

Following longer sequences of pattern instructions

yarn

Rowan Baby Merino Silk DK, (66% wool, 34% silk) light worsted (DK) yarn

6 x 1¾ oz (50 g) balls—882 yd (810 m) —of shade 695 Candy (A)

1 x 1¾ oz (50 g) ball—147 yd (135 m)— of shade 670 Snowdrop (B)

needles

Pair of US size 6 (4 mm) needles

other materials

Blunt darning needle

finished measurements

Length: 20 in. (50 cm) square

Around neckline: 24 in. (60 cm)

gauge (tension)

Before blocking: 22 sts and 30 rows to 4 in. (10 cm) working stockinette (stocking) stitch using US size 6 (4 mm) needles.

After blocking: 20 sts and 32 rows to 4 in. (10 cm) working stockinette (stocking) stitch using US size 6 (4 mm) needles.

abbreviations

k	knit
k2tog	knit 2 stitches together
LH	left-hand
p	purl
patt	pattern
rep	repeat
sl	slip
st(s)	stitch(es)
WS	wrong side
yo	yarn over

Special abbreviation

wrap and sl next st – bring yarn to front, sl next st, take yarn to back.

Special note:

You will find that when changing yarns you will sometimes need to break and rejoin the yarn using the technique learned in Workshop 6 (see page 65). Do not carry the yarns up the side of the work for this project, because the edges need to look neat at both sides.

To make the wrap
Using yarn A, cast on 100 sts.
Row 1 (WS): K to end.
Row 2: As Row 1.
Row 3: As Row 1.
Row 4: Change to yarn B, k to end.
Row 5: K to end.
Row 6: Change to yarn A, k to end.
Row 7: K to end.
***Row 8:** K2, [yo, k2tog] to last 2 sts, k2.
Row 9: K to end.
Row 10: Change to yarn B, k to end.
Row 11: K to end.
Row 12: Change to yarn A, k to end.
Rows 13–15: K to end.

Aftercare

To wear the wrap, throw it over your shoulders and clasp it closed with a decorative brooch or pin.

Hand wash the piece and dry it flat to avoid distortion.

Panel:
Row 16: K39, wrap and sl next st, turn.
Row 17: With yarn in front, sl wrapped st, p35, k4, turn.
Row 18: K37, wrap and sl next st, turn.
Row 19: Sl wrapped st, p33, k4, turn.
Row 20: K35, wrap and sl next st, turn.
Row 21: Sl wrapped st, p31, k4, turn.
Row 22: K33, wrap and sl next st, turn.
Row 23: Sl wrapped st, p29, k4, turn.
Row 24: K31, wrap and sl next st, turn.
Row 25: Sl wrapped st, p27, k4, turn.
Row 26: K29, wrap and sl next st, turn.
Row 27: Sl wrapped st, p25, k4, turn.
Row 28: K27, wrap and sl next st, turn.
Row 29: Sl wrapped st, p23, k4, turn.
Row 30: K25, wrap and sl next st, turn.
Row 31: Sl wrapped st, p21, k4, turn.
Row 32: K23, wrap and sl next st, turn.
Row 33: Sl wrapped st, p19, k4, turn.
Row 34: K21, wrap and sl next st, turn.
Row 35: Sl wrapped st, p17, k4, turn.
Row 36: K19, wrap and sl next st, turn.
Row 37: Sl wrapped st, p15, k4, turn.
Row 38: K17, wrap and sl next st, turn.
Row 39: Sl wrapped st, p13, k4, turn.
Row 40: K15, wrap and sl next st, turn.
Row 41: Sl wrapped st, p11, k4, turn.
Row 42: K13, wrap and sl next st, turn.
Row 43: Sl wrapped st, p9, k4, turn.
Row 44: K11, wrap and sl next st, turn.
Row 45: Sl wrapped st, p7, k4, turn.
Row 46: K9, wrap and sl next st, turn.
Row 47: Sl wrapped st, p5, k4, turn.
Row 48: K7, wrap and sl next st, turn.
Row 49: Sl wrapped st, p3, k4, turn.
Row 50: K5, wrap and sl next st, turn.
Row 51: Sl wrapped st, p1, k4, turn.
Row 52: K to end, working as follows for every wrapped st: k wrapped st then lift wrap onto LH needle and knit tog with next st (as a k2tog).
This 52-row sequence forms patt and completes first panel. Work a second panel as set, but for Row 8 use the alternative instructions below, so the piece does not slant in one direction:
***Alternative Row 8:** K2, [k2tog, yo] to last 2 sts, k2.
Work a further 13 panels, using Row 8 on panels 3, 5, 7, 9, 11, and 13 and Alternative Row 8 on panels 4, 6, 8, 10, and 12. Bind (cast) off.

Finishing
Weave in all loose yarn tails neatly (see Workshop 1, page 25). Block the piece carefully so the fluted panels maintain their dimensional quality and edges lie flat. You may need to gently press the piece under a damp dish towel, but use a cool iron to protect the fibers. If possible, try to block using the steam method alone (see Workshop 1, Blocking, page 26).

Casting on extra stitches at the end of a row
Place the needle with all the stitches on it in your left hand, and work as if you were at the start of the next row.

Casting on extra stitches in the middle of a row
You may need to cast on extra stitches in the middle of a row, to create a 3-D effect, or as part of the construction of a buttonhole. In the project for this workshop, the central opening of the peg bag is constructed using this method. To achieve this, work along the row to the point where you want to cast on the stitches, swap your needles over to use the one containing all the stitches just worked as your left needle, and then follow the method shown opposite until you have cast on as many stitches as you need. Switch the needles back around and continue as you were to the end of your row.

Working extra sti

Sometimes these extra
the first row, particular
experience this, pull ge
left thumb as you work
slide your needle in to

Holding stitches

You may wonder why you would to need to hold some stitches while you work on others. Now that you understand short rowing it might seem that employing this technique will cover many tricky shaping situations, but once you begin to create knitted pieces that call for symmetrical shaping within a piece you will need to widen your repertoire of skills—especially if you want a professional finish.

The most comm
stitches is when ma
Because the neckli
possible to knit it
knit each side sepa
detail in Workshop
project in this wor
holding stitches an
a few rows to creat

Three ways to hold stitches
There are several ways to hold stitches until you need to work them, so you can choose which one suits a particular circumstance..

Leaving held stitches on the needle
You learned in Short Rowing (see page 73) that you can leave stitches not being worked on the needle until they are worked back into the piece. Essentially, this is the same technique as holding stitches. For some patterns, where the hold only lasts for a few rows, or when it is staggered and each stitch is held for one row longer than its neighbor—as in the Short-row Wrap in Workshop 8—then this works fine. The stitches can withstand the extra tension put on them while they are held because it is not too substantial. Therefore for some projects leaving the stitches not being worked just sitting idle on the needle is fully acceptable.

The method employed in these cases is to complete the first side, bind (cast) it off, then re-attach the yarn to the piece and complete the remaining side. You might also be asked to bind (cast) off stitches in the middle—this is straightforward and in this method should be done after working the first side so that the yarn is carried with you to the remaining side.

Workshop 9

Shaping and using gauge/

In Workshop 8 we looked at turning before the end of a row and continuing to knit to create a shaped piece, but there are other knitting techniques that involve interrupting a normal row to alter the shape. In this workshop we look at how to hold stitches while working on another part of the row,

how to cast on
middle of a ro
the middle of
uses all these t
Peg Bag. We al
when you use
one recommer

Casting on extra stitches

Back in Workshop 5, you learned that you can increase one or two stitches by working two or three times into the same stitch (see page 52). The M1 method (see Workshop 10, page 88) also allows you to increase by one stitch at a time. But if you want to increase several stitches at a time, the only way is to cast on stitches at the beginning or end of

a row. This make
there are times v
needed—it is rai
required. In the
92), you need to
some of the glov
of when this tec

Casting on extra stitches at the beginning of a row
This is not as difficult as it might sound. It employs the cable method of cast on, which we learne
Getting Started (see page 16).

1 Hold your needles and work as if you were beginning the next row as normal. Knit the first stitch, but do not drop it off the left needle yet.

2 Transfer the new stitch you have just created back onto the left needle, by inserting the left needle into it from front to back and from right to left. Then remove it from the right needle—this is your first new cast-on stitch.

Fabric lining for knitted items
It's not necessary to line most knitted items, but yarn can be stretchy so adding a fabric lining will strengthen bags and purses and help them to hold their shape. The sewing skills required are only very basic.

Lining a bag
These general instructions will allow you to line most items, but some of the projects with lining have additional techniques (see pages 87 and 105).

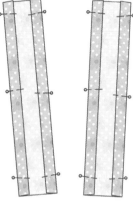

1 If the item has straps or a handle to be lined, measure the knitted strips and cut the lining fabric an extra ⅝ in. (1.5 cm) wider on each side to allow for the hem.

2 Press a ⅝-in. (1.5-cm) wide hem to the wrong side along each long edge of the fabric strips and pin in place.

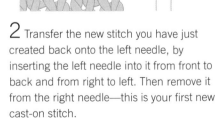

3 Place the lining with the hem side down onto the wrong side of each knitted strip. Pin and then hand sew the lining to the edge of the knitting using oversewing (see page 27). Remove the pins.

4 To position a pair of handles on a knitted bag, first make up the bag by stitching the side seams. Place a pin marker approximately 1 in. (2.5 cm) in from each outside seam along the top edge of the bag, on both the front and the back.

5 With the knitted side of the handle to the inside of the bag, attach the ends of the first handle so that they extend down into the bag by about 2 in. (5 cm), with the outer edge of each handle to a pin marker. Pin in place and then hand sew the handle to the bag. Repeat on the other side of the bag to add the other handle and then remove any remaining pins.

Choosing a lining fabric

When using the knitted piece as a pattern to measure the size of fabric to cut for the lining, it's best to block the knitting first so that it's the correct size and shape.

If the knitting is intended to be washable, make sure that the lining fabric is both washable and colorfast.

Choose a lining fabric that tones with your knitting; go darker rather than lighter because light or bright colors are more likely to show through open knitted fabrics.

Unless otherwise directed in the pattern, choose a woven fabric rather than a knitted jersey. The rigidity of a woven fabric adds stability to stretchy knitting, which is useful for items that may be pulled, such as bags.

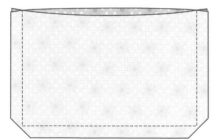

6 Lay the knitted bag flat and use it as a pattern to cut two pieces of lining fabric to the same size plus an extra ⅝ in. (1.5 cm) allowance for seams on the sides and bottom and an extra 1 in. (2.5 cm) at the top. Pin the fabric pieces right sides together and machine sew the side and bottom seams. Trim across the bottom corners and press the seams.

7 Turn the top edge of the lining over to the wrong side by 1 in. (2.5 cm) and press.

8 Insert the lining into the bag with wrong sides together and pin in place around the top edge. Hand sew the lining to the knitting around the top edge, stitching across the handles again for extra security.

Peg bag

By working on smaller needles a sturdy, durable fabric is produced for this useful peg bag, designed by Pauline Richards. It is knitted in one piece with an oval-shaped opening, and features daisy stitch, which is a lovely, interesting stitch to have in your repertoire. A gently curved or straight wooden clothes hanger is needed to hang your peg bag—use a child's hanger or cut a larger one down to size using a small hack saw.

techniques used

Casting on

Increasing by knitting into front and back of stitch

Decreasing using k2tog

Shaping by binding (casting) off in center of a row

Holding stitches

Daisy stitch

Backstitch to join

Oversewing

yarn

Rowan All Seasons Cotton (60% cotton/40% acrylic) worsted (Aran) yarn

3 x 1¾ oz (50 g) balls—294 yd (270 m) —of shade 255 Summer (A)

1 x 1¾ oz (50 g) ball—98 yd (90 m)—of shade 253 Fez (B)

needles

Pair of US size 6 (4 mm) needles

other materials

Stitch holder

Blunt darning needle

Sewing needle and thread to match fabric

12 x 24 in. (30 x 61 cm) of cotton lining fabric

11 in. (28 cm) curved or straight wooden clothes hanger

finished measurements

12 x 11 in. (30 x 28 cm)

gauge (tension)

25 sts and 27 rows to 4 in. (10 cm) working daisy stitch using US size 6 (4 mm) needles.

abbreviations

cont	continue
inc	increase by knitting into front and back of same stitch
k	knit
k2tog	knit 2 stitches together
LH	left-hand
p	purl
patt	pattern
rem	remains
RH	right-hand
RS	right side
st(s)	stitch(es)
tog	together
WS	wrong side
yrn	yarn round needle
[]	repeat sequence within square brackets the number of times indicated

Special abbreviation

Daisy st (Daisy stitch) – p next 3 sts tog but do not let them drop from needle, yrn, p the same 3 sts tog, now drop them from LH needle, k1.

To make the bag

Using yarn A and the cable method, cast on 73 sts.
Rows 1 and 3 (RS): K to end.
Row 2: K1, [Daisy st] to end.
Row 4: K1, p1, k1, [Daisy st] to last 2 sts, p1, k1.
These 4 rows set patt.
Cont in patt until 112 rows have been worked.
Change to yarn B and continue in patt for 15 rows.
Shape opening:
Next row: K1, p1, k1, [Daisy st] 4 times, p2, bind (cast) off 31 sts (1 st rem on RH needle), p1, k1, [Daisy st] 4 times, p1, k1.
Cont on last 21 sts only, leaving first 21 sts on needle.
Next row: K19, k2tog.
Next row: K2tog, p1, k1, [Daisy st] 4 times.
Next row: K17, k2tog.

Next row: K2tog, p1, k1, [Daisy st] 3 times, p1, k1.
Next row: K17.
Next row: Inc in next st, [Daisy st] 4 times.
Next row: K18, inc in next st.
Next row: Inc in next st, [Daisy st] 4 times, p1, k1.
Next row: K19, inc in next st.
Break yarn and place 21 sts on st holder. Rejoin yarn to opening edge of LH side and cont on these 21 sts.
Next row: K2tog, k19.
Next row: K1, [Daisy st] 4 times, p1, k2tog.
Next row: K2tog, k17.
Next row: K1, p1, k1, [Daisy st] 3 times, p1, k2tog.
Next row: K17.
Next row: K1, [Daisy st] 4 times, inc in last k st of patt.
Next row: Inc in next st, k17.
Next row: K1, p1, k1, [Daisy st] 4 times, inc in last st of patt.

Next row: Inc in next st, k19.

Next row: K1, [Daisy st] 5 times, turn, cast on 31 sts using cable method, turn, working across held sts on RH side of opening, k1, [Daisy st] 5 times.

Next row: K to end.

Cont in patt for 14 more rows, ending with a K row.

Bind (cast) off.

Finishing

Press lightly on the WS using a pressing cloth or dish towel.

Lay knitting onto lining fabric and use as a template to mark a hole for the opening that is ⅜ in. (1 cm) smaller than the opening all round to allow for a seam allowance. Cut out the hole and snip into the seam allowance so it will lie flat.

Making up

Fold lining in half with RS facing and sew side seams, leaving top edge open.

Fold peg bag in half with RS facing. Using yarn A, sew side seams using backstitch (see page 33). Turn RS out.

Place lining inside peg bag with WS together, aligning openings and turning in seam allowance on lining. Slipstitch together around opening using matching sewing thread.

Sew along top of lining, leaving a small gap at center for hanger hook to go through. Oversew top of peg bag with yarn B, again leaving a gap for hook. Insert clothes hanger through front opening and thread hook through gap left at the top.

Sponge clean only.

Workshop 10

Picking up stitches and making extra stitches

We have learned several shaping techniques, but there is one more common way of increasing to learn: make 1. Sometimes you will need to start knitting in part of the piece other than the working row—in this workshop you will also learn how to pick up stitches and later workshops will develop this further. The project in this workshop is a pair of Fluted Gloves, which will put into practice many of the techniques learned so far.

Increasing by make 1 method (M1)

This is a neat way of increasing and good to use in finer items, where the quality of the gauge (tension) and stitches really shows. Now that you are well used to examining your knitted fabric in terms of qualities, and being able to spot changes of direction, you should be able to locate the necessary loop to work this stitch. To practice this and the next skill, make a piece of stockinette (stocking) stitch that is approximately 20 stitches and 10 rows.

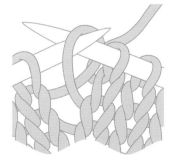

Working in stockinette (stocking) stitch, and on the knit side of the fabric, knit the first couple of stitches as normal. Find the horizontal strand of yarn that lies between the stitch you have just knitted and the next one on the left-hand needle. Pick this strand up onto your left needle, inserting it from front to back. Now knit into the back of this stitch, rather than the front as you usually would—if you knit into the front you will produce a hole, but the twist produced by knitting into the back avoids this.

Picking up stitches

Being able to pick up and create stitches at various places within knitting is a great skill to learn. It offers great scope for three-dimensional work and is a vital skill when tackling garments—it can help you create quite complex shapes, add edgings and borders, and knit pieces at different angles. If you eventually start to create your own knitting patterns and designs you can use this skill to avoid excess seams and produce very professional results.

Picking up stitches along a horizontal edge

First we will cover various ways to pick up and work stitches horizontally. You need this technique in order to work the gloves in the project that follows. The phrase "pick up" stitches usually means "pick up and knit"; you may see that written out, or perhaps "knit up"—all three phrases mean the same thing. Essentially you are making new, active stitches from a completed or bound (cast) off piece or edge. Whenever you pick up stitches you should never take the very edge loops, because this will look untidy, full of holes, and may become baggy. It is far better to take the next loop—or even the next stitch—inward, even though doing so may make for a slightly thicker seam.

The most straightforward way of picking up stitches is when you pick up the same number of stitches as there are in the piece, in a horizontal direction, and at the top of the piece. For example, if you are making a garment you will often have to pick up stitches from the top of the back piece when you knit the neckline: this will tend to be a straight line with one stitch picked up per knitted stitch of the piece. In such cases one shoulder may be sewn up first, with a given number of stitches in the center to be picked up for the neckline.

Picking up stitches along the top of a piece of knitting

First make a simple piece of knitting in stockinette (stocking) stitch, of at least 20 stitches and 20 rows. Bind (cast) off. Lightly press it with an iron so that it lies flat and you can see the edge stitches easily—this is one of the few times you will be asked to place an iron on the knitting!

Take a contrasting color of yarn, so that you can easily see it, and tension it in your hands ready to use. Hold the piece of knitting in your left hand, knit side facing you, and insert the right needle in through the center of the first stitch, directly below the bound (cast) off edge and not in the edge chain itself. Place the needle right through the central V. Wrap the yarn around the needle and pull back through so that you have created a new loop on the needle.

Repeat for each stitch along the row (A). You should have picked up and knitted 20 new stitches, which are now active and ready to work with. If you were knitting a neckline, these would form your first row or round. Bear in mind that, if you wish to maintain the continuity of the stockinette (stocking) stitch and have the knit side of the new piece carry on from the knit side of the old piece, then your first row worked will be a purl one using this method.

An alternative method for this type of picking up stitches includes using a crochet hook instead of a knitting needle (B), and then transferring the stitches back onto a knitting needle as you go along. This may be a useful skill to try when you have a spare moment, because very occasionally you might need to pick up stitches from left to right and this is far less counter-intuitive than using a knitting needle backward if you are right handed.

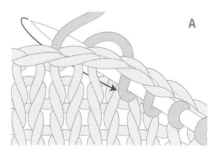

A

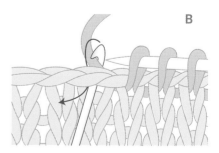

B

Picking up stitches from the center of a piece of knitting

There may be times when you wish to start creating a new piece of knitting from within an existing one, but not at the edge. For instance, if you decide to add a pocket in to a garment that is already finished, this is a possible solution.

Use the crochet method on page 89, following along the row carefully. You might find it useful to thread a piece of contrast yarn through along the row you wish to pick up before you start, to help you stay straight. Again, your first row will be a purl row if you are maintaining the flow of stockinette (stocking) stitch. Try it out on the test piece of knitting you used above.

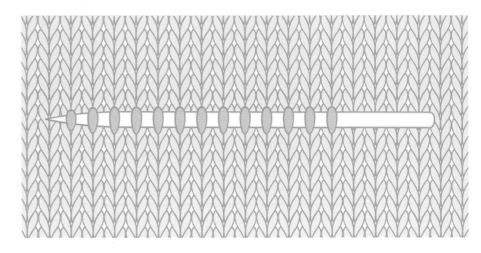

Picking up stitches from the bottom

This is relatively unusual but it does crop up in the project that follows—you need to be able to pick up stitches from the cast-on edge of the fingers to create room for movement between fingers. The technique of making the stitches is basically the same, but you turn the work upside down so that the bottom edge is at the top. The stitches are also effectively upside down now, so you must bear this in mind and treat the stitches as upside down Vs in order to be able to see where to insert your needle to pick up a new stitch. It will look as if you are working into the running threads rather than the Vs themselves.

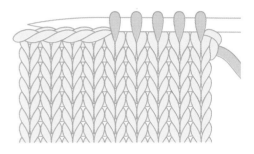

Picking up stitches along a vertical edge

Another common technique, this is employed to make the button bands of cardigans (see Workshop 20, College Cardigan, page 167), within the construction of some necklines, and to edge blankets or throws. It has an added complication in that you cannot simply pick up one stitch for every row, unless your pattern advises this, because knitted stitches are not square; the width exceeds the length—we will investigate this further when we work with charts in later workshops. If, for example, the top and bottom each measure ⅜ in. (1 cm) and the sides measure ⁹⁄₃₂ in. (7 mm), a panel of 20 sts and 20 rows would measure 8 in. (20 cm) by 5½ in. (14 cm). So, if you picked up one stitch for every row along one side edge, you would pick up 20 stitches, which measures 8 in. (20 cm) in this example—but you only have a 5½ in. (14 cm) edge. So although it is physically possible to pick up 20 stitches, the result

Picking up stitches in a curve

On a neckline you will often have to pick up stitches in a combination of horizontal, vertical, and curved or diagonal orientation because the shape of the front neckline, in particular, may be quite deeply curved. Again, your knitting pattern will tell you how many stitches to pick up in each area, so for the horizontal and vertical picking up follow the instructions above. In Workshop 12 we will look at how to deal with diagonal or curved areas when working a neckline.

would be either a very puckered piece of knitting or a very stretched out and distorted edge. So you need to reduce the number of stitches picked up so that they fit comfortably into the edge and achieve the desired effect, be it flat or evenly gathered.

Knitting pattern instructions will always tell you how many stitches to pick up along an edge—what you have to do is work out how often to skip a row when picking up to create a smooth edge. As a general rule, picking up two or three stitches then skipping one will often produce the right number of stitches. In the example given earlier, you need to pick up 14 stitches over 20 rows, so you need to skip six rows during your picking up. If you skip roughly one row every three pick-ups you will have picked up 14 stitches by the end of the seam.

Picking up stitches along a side

Hold the piece with the knit side facing and rotated so that the bottom edge is on the right. Insert your needle into the running thread between the first and second stitches of the first row, and knit it up—this is your first stitch. Work along the same column of running threads, remembering to skip a row every three or four pick-ups, or as the pattern suggests.

When working this technique in garter stitch or seed (moss) stitch, you can pick up loops a little closer to the edge because the bumps on the purl stitches will not create such a visible seam as in stockinette (stocking) stitch.

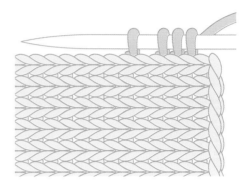

Putting your skills into practice

You have extended your knitting skills considerably within this workshop and you are ready tackle the project that follows—a pair of gloves, knitted in finer yarn and thinner needles than we have worked with until now. You will have a chance to practice your shaping skills, as well as making stitches, casting on at the end of rows, picking up stitches, and mattress stitch. At this point in the book, you can feel confident that you will be able to produce a well-finished, refined item that shows off your abilities in luxurious yarn.

Fluted gloves

These luxuriously soft, draped gloves are quite unusual in that they are knitted on two needles rather than four double-pointed needles. The fluted shape of the cuff is achieved through use of knit and purl stitches in a ribbing pattern that changes as it is decreased, producing a godet shape. You can wear the cuff folded back or left long to fit under coat sleeves. The fine needles and yarn used may seem a little daunting, but remember that this is a small, portable project—and once you have made the first glove, the second one will be easy!

techniques used

Increasing using M1

Decreasing using k2tog

Increasing by casting on at the end of a row

Holding stitches

Picking up stitches to reknit

Mattress stitch to join

yarn

Drops Baby Alpaca silk (70% alpaca/30%silk) fingering (4-ply) yarn

1 x 1¾ oz (50 g) ball—182 yd (167 m)—each of shade 6347 Blue Purple (A) and shade 7219 Pistachio (B)

needles

Pair of US size 2 (2.75 mm) needles for size small–medium gloves OR

Pair of US size 3 (3.25 mm) needles for size medium–large gloves

other materials

Blunt darning needle

finished measurements

To fit small–medium(**medium–large**) female hands

Finished measurements:

Length from cuff to fingertips: 10½ in./27 cm (**12¼ in./31 cm**)

Width of hand at wrist: 6 in./15 cm (**6½ in./16.5 cm**)

gauge (tension)

32 sts and 39 rows to 4 in. (10 cm) square working stockinette (stocking) stitch using US size 2 (2.75 mm) needles for small–medium size.

29 sts and 34 rows to 4 in. (10 cm) square working stockinette (stocking) stitch using US size 3 (3.25 mm) for medium–large size.

abbreviations

beg	beginning
k	knit
k2tog	knit 2 stitches together
LH	left-hand
M1	increase by picking up and knitting loop between current and next stitch
p	purl
sts	stitch(es)
st st	stockinette (stocking) stitch
rep	repeat
RH	right-hand
RS	right side
WS	wrong side
[]	repeat sequence within square brackets the number of times indicated

Right glove

*Using yarn A and thumb method (see page 163), cast on 96 sts.
Row 1 (RS): K to end.
Row 2 (WS): Rep row 1.
Row 3: Rep Row 1
Row 4: Rep Row 1.
Row 5: K1, p6, [k2, p6] 11 times, k1.
Row 6: P1, k6, [p2, k6] 11 times, p1.
Change to yarn B.

Row 7: Rep Row 5.
Row 8: Rep Row 6.
Change to yarn A.
Row 9: Rep Row 5.
Row 10: P1, k2tog, k2, k2tog, [p2, k2tog, k2, k2tog] 11 times, p1. 72 sts
Row 11: K1, p4, [k2, p4] 11 times, k1.
Row 12: P1, k4, [p2, k4] 11 times, p1.
Change to yarn B.
Rows 13 and 15: Rep Row 11.

Row 14: Rep Row 12.
Row 16: P1, k2tog, k2tog [p2, k2tog, k2tog] 11 times, p1. 48 sts
Change to yarn A.
Row 17: K1, p2, [k2, p2] 11 times, k1.
Row 18: P1, k2, [p2, k2] 11 times, p1.
Change to yarn B.
Rows 19, 21, and 23: Rep Row 17.
Rows 20, 22, and 24: Rep Row 18.
Change to yarn A.
Row 25: Rep Row 17.
Row 26: Rep Row 18.
Change to yarn B.
Work 6 rows in st st, beg with a k row. **
Begin shaping thumb:
Next row: K27, M1, k1, M1, k to end.
Work 3 rows in st st.
Next row: K27, M1, k3, M1, k to end.
Work 3 rows in st st, beg with a p row.
Next row: K27, M1, k5, M1, k to end.
Work 3 rows in st st, beg with a p row.
Next row: K27, M1, k7, M1, k to end.
Work 3 rows in st st, beg with a p row.
Next row: K27, M1, k9, M1, k to end.
Work 3 rows in st st, beg with a p row.
Next row: K27, M1, k11, M1, k to end.
Work 5 rows in st st, beg with a p row. 60 sts
Work thumb:
Next row: K40, turn.
Next row: P13, cast on 4 sts, turn. (17 sts)
Now work 20 rows in st st, beg with a k row.

Shape thumb top:
Next row: K2tog, [k1, k2tog] 5 times.
Next row: P11.
Next row: [K2tog] 5 times, k1.
Next row: P6.
Break yarn and thread tail into a blunt darning needle; thread this through all rem sts on the needle, pushing them off the needle as you go, then pull tight to close up. Join seam using mattress stitch (see page 55).
***With RS facing, join yarn in last st on RH needle. Pick up and knit (see page 90) the 4 sts cast on at base of thumb, picking up one extra loop as you go, to make 5 sts in all (it is easier to pick up the loops at the bottom of the knitting), k across sts on LH needle. 52 sts
Work 17 rows in st st, beg with a p row. ***
First finger:
Next row: K34, turn.
Next row: P15, cast on 2 sts, turn.
Work 22 rows in st st, starting with a k row.
Shape top:
Next row: [K2, k2tog] 4 times, k1.
Next row: P13.
Next row: [K1, k2tog] 4 times, k1.
Next row: P9.
Complete as for thumb, threading rem sts through and drawing up to close.
Second finger:
Next row: With RS facing, join yarn in last st on RH needle, then pick up and knit 2 sts cast on at base of first finger, picking up one extra loop as you go, to make 3 sts in all (the extra stitch created makes space between fingers, so the gloves sit comfortably), k7, turn.
Next row: P17, cast on 2 sts, turn.
Work 24 rows in st st, beg with a k row.
Shape top:
Next row: [K2, k2tog] 4 times, k3.
Next row: P15.
Next row: [K1, k2tog] 5 times.
Next row: P10.
Complete as for thumb, threading rem sts through and drawing up to close.
Third finger:
Next row: With RS facing, join yarn in last st on RH needle, then pick up and knit 2 sts cast on at base of second finger, picking up one extra loop as you go, to make 3 sts in all, k6, turn.
Next row: P16, cast on 2 sts, turn.
Now work 22 rows in st st, beg with a k row.
Shape top:
Next row: [K2, k2tog] 4 times, k2.
Next row: P14.
Next row: [K1, k2tog] 4 times, k2.
Next row: P10.
Complete as for thumb, threading rem sts through and drawing up to close.

Fourth finger:
Next row: With RS facing, join yarn in last st on RH needle, then pick up and knit 2 sts cast on at base of third finger, picking up one extra loop as you go to make 3 sts in all, k5, turn.
Next row: P13.
Now work 16 rows in st st, beg with a k row.
Shape top:
Next row: [K1, k2tog] 4 times, k1.
Next row: P9.
Next row: [K2tog] 4 times, k1.
Next row: P5.
Complete as for thumb but leaving a much longer yarn tail so that you can stitch all down side of glove to join it up.

Left glove
Work as for Right Glove from * to **.
Begin shaping thumb:
Next row: K20, M1, k1, M1, k to end.
Work 3 rows in st st, beg with a p row.
Next row: K20, M1, k3, M1, k to end.
Work 3 rows in st st, beg with a p row.
Next row: K20, M1, k5, M1, k to end.
Work 3 rows in st st, beg with a p row.
Next row: K20, M1, k7, M1, k to end.
Work 3 rows in st st, beg with a p row.
Next row: K20, M1, k9, M1, k to end.
Work 3 rows in st st, beg with a p row.
Next row: K20, M1, k11, M1, k to end.
Work 5 rows in st st, beg with a p row.

Work thumb:
Next row: K33, cast on 4 sts, turn.
Next row: P17.
Complete as for thumb of Right Glove.
Work as for Right Glove from *** to ***.
First finger:
Next row: K33, cast on 2 sts, turn.
Next row: P17, turn.
Complete as for first finger of Right Glove.
Second finger:
Next row: With RS facing, join yarn in last st on RH needle, pick up and knit the 2 sts cast on at base of first finger, picking up an extra loop as you go so that you have 3 sts in total, k7, cast on 2 sts, turn.
Next row: P19, turn.
Complete as for second finger of Right Glove.
Third finger:
Next row: With RS facing, join yarn in last st on RH needle, pick up and knit the 2 sts cast on at base of second finger, picking up an extra loop as you go so that you have 3 sts in total, k7, cast on 2 sts, turn.
Next row: P18, turn.
Complete as for third finger of Right Glove.
Fourth finger:
Complete fourth finger and rest of glove as for Right Glove.

Making up
Weave in all loose tails (see Workshop 1, page 25). Steam the gloves lightly, but do not press them because this would remove the soft pile of the yarn.

Aftercare
Hand launder your gloves and dry them flat.

Workshop 11

Working cables, crossing stitches, and introducing symbols

We have been through the building blocks of knitting; now we add intermediate level techniques to enhance your work. In this workshop we learn to cross stitches over each other to create simple textures, cables, and lattices. We also start looking at charts, as used in modern knitting patterns, and also how the information is given in vintage, longhand traditional patterns so you will have the skills to follow both methods. The project for this workshop, a Messenger Bag, puts several cabling variations into practice.

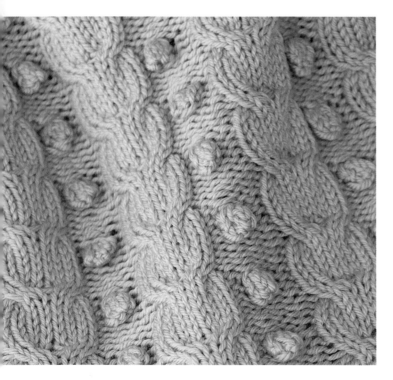

Traditional patterns

When many people conjure up an image of "complicated" knitting they think of a cabled Aran sweater, or perhaps an intricately-colored Fair Isle piece. Because these traditional patterns have been around for centuries, and many of us will have received such garments lovingly crafted by doting grandparents or aunts, we have a reverence for the techniques that might make us rather afraid to tackle them. It is true that neither technique is quickly worked, nor can be knitted without a certain level of concentration and commitment. However, both are quite straightforward to learn once you have mastered the basics of knitting itself.

Besides being highly decorative, cabled knitting is also warm and thick. This is one of the reasons it has been popular in fishing communities, because the added warmth given by many columns of cables was invaluable to those out at sea in atrocious weather conditions. When knitted in untreated wool these sweaters were also impressively waterproof, because the copious lanolin in the fleece provided resistance to the rain and sea spray. There is some opinion that many traditional cable patterns represented villages, surnames, number of children, and suchlike, so that should a sailor be lost at sea his body could be identified by his sweater if necessary. This may be folklore—but it certainly adds to the charm of these striking patterns.

Cables

A cable is the term given to a series of stitches crossed over each other, so groups of stitches are worked in a different order. If you want to change the order of more than two stitches you have to put one group of stitches "on hold" on a cable needle, which is a small extra knitting needle with a point at each end, while you knit the other group.

Most of us will be familiar with the rope-like patterns on cricket sweaters and the intricate, woolen knitting designs of the Aran isles off mainland Ireland. Some of these structures are incredibly detailed, with the "ropes" being intertwined and threading in and out of each other multiple times. Each time the "rope" twists in the design, the stitches within the rope in that row are crossed over each other. In lattice patterns the cabling might occur in a more subtle way, with the stitches appearing to travel diagonally over a larger area. Again, the cable needle is employed to work this maneuver.

The technique consists of two types of move: the stitches are either crossed over each other in the front, or at the back. Everything else is a variation on this: the number of stitches in the cable, the number of rows between each cross, the sequence of crosses—once you have learned the basic moves you can extend your knowledge of cabling by trying out many permutations of the technique.

Crossed stitches

When only one stitch is crossed over another, there is no need to use a separate cable needle. It can help to go up a size in knitting needles, because the yarn is required to repeatedly extend itself in the crossed stitches and so might lose some of its elasticity. Some textural patterns employ this technique.

Basic crossed stitch (worked on the knit side)

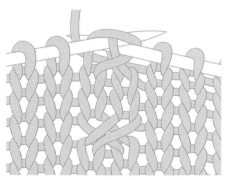

To cross two stitches, insert the right needle into the second stitch along on the left needle, going in from front to back. Knit this stitch, but do not push any stitches off the left needle yet. Next, knit the first stitch on the left needle, and then push both stitches off the left needle at once. You will see that a tiny cross has been created. Although very subtle, this pattern looks effective and pretty when repeated.

If you wish to cross on the purl side of the fabric, you simply purl the stitches instead of knitting them.

General rules for cables

Cable patterns that form a rope pattern usually consist of two equal groups of stitches—for example, a 6-stitch cable will be made up of two groups of three stitches and an 8-stitch cable consists of two groups of four stitches.

Rope cable patterns also only require the stitches to be crossed every six to ten rows, on average. This does not have to be the case—and many patterns will vary from this—but enough straight rows must be worked between the cables for the pattern to have impact and curve.

Cables can be worked twisting to the left or to the right, the difference being achieved by placing the cable needle at the front or the back of the work accordingly. They tend always to be worked on the knit side of the fabric, with the adjacent stitches being in reverse stockinette (stocking) stitch (purl side facing). This enhances the dimensional quality of the cables because the background recedes further, pushing the cables upward.

Choosing a cable needle

It is helpful to use a cable needle that is a little bit thinner than your knitting needles. This is because the stitches have to move, and they will have a little bit more "give" if they are held by a thinner diameter needle. Cable needles are often sold in packs of two: one thick and one thin. Some of them are completely straight, and some have a kink in the center, which makes it easier to hold the stitches on them. For most knitting, two cable needles are all you will ever need.

Working with a cable needle

When moving stitches to cross them, the stitches that are to be physically moved are placed on the cable needle, which is then either left at the front of the work, or at the back. It can feel a little precarious to have stitches sitting unsecured on this separate needle, particularly if the cable needle is straight; one knock with your hand and they could slide off. To counteract this, I always push the left-hand tip of the cable needle down into the knitting, so that the right-hand end sticks upward at an angle of approximately 45°, which keeps the stitches in place. When it is time to knit the stitches off the cable needle it is released from the fabric. Alternatively, you can use a cable needle that has a kink in it.

Left cross cable (cabling in front/front cable)
To practice this technique, you will need a cable needle thinner in gauge than the knitting needles you are using.

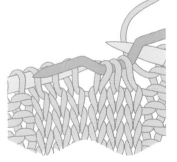 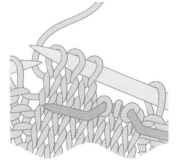 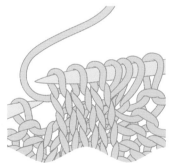

Cast on 30 sts and knit 10 rows as follows:
Row 1: P6, [k6, p6] twice.
Row 2: k6, [p6, k6] twice.
Repeat Rows 1 and 2 four more times. (10 rows worked)

Row 11 (cable row): P6, *slip the next three stitches onto the cable needle purlwise, and leave it at the front of the work.

Now, knit the next stitch off the left needle. Tighten the yarn slightly, then knit the next two stitches on the left needle.

Finally knit the first stitch off the cable needle. Tighten the yarn a little, then knit the remaining two stitches off the cable needle. P6, rep from * once more.

Work Row 2 once again.
Work Rows 1 and 2 four more times each, then stop to examine your work. You should see a clear cable crossed toward the left, over each of the two bands of knit stitches.
Work Row 11 once again, then Row 2 once, then Rows 1 and 2 four more times again.

If you feel you need more practice, continue in this way until you feel happy you are able to cable in front, to the left. Once you are happy, move on to working a right cross cable.

Right cross cable (cabling at back/back cable)

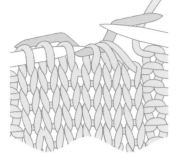 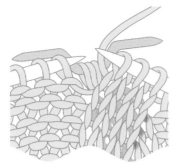 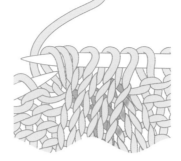

Next row (cable row): P6, *slip the next three stitches onto the cable needle purlwise, and hold it at the back of the work.

Knit the next stitch off the left needle, tighten the yarn a little, and then knit the next two stitches off the left needle.

Next, knit the first stitch off the cable needle, tighten the yarn slightly, then knit the remaining two stitches off the cable needle. P6, rep from * once more.

Work Row 2 once again and then Rows 1 and 2 four more times each, then work the cable row again, then Row 2 again, and finally Rows 1 and 2 four more times. You should see two clear cable bands that twist toward the right on their last two turns.

By alternating the direction of the twist, and varying the number of rows between cables, it is possible to create an intricate design. As with slip stitch there are an enormous number of cable patterns—a good pattern directory book will increase your repertoire. For the moment spend some time creating varied samples of your own—try making cables with 4, 8, and 10 stitches, and working them to the right and to the left. Place two cables adjacent to each other and work one to the right, and one to the left.

Hopefully now you are beginning to see the potential of this technique. The project that follows focuses on teaching many cable variations, while the Funnel Neck Sweater in Workshop 12 (see page 112) gives you a chance to work a stunning, large-scale lattice cable as the centerpiece of a garment.

Lattice patterns

Besides the very familiar rope patterns, cable techniques are used to make lattice-type patterns. Worked in exactly the same way, but with more frequent cabling and relatively narrow cables, these are intricate and stunning, if a little slow to work. Lattice patterns tend to have a single, narrow cable traveling over a reverse stockinette (stocking) stitch ground: when working this type of pattern you will find that you often have to purl the stitch that the knit cable is traveling over or under, to maintain the contrast between the two stitch types. The Funnel Neck Sweater project in Workshop 12 (see page 112) uses this type of cabling.

Introducing charts

Charts are a relatively modern innovation in the art of knitting-pattern writing. If you are someone who learns in a very visual way, they will appeal to you immediately. The prospect of seeing an entire sweater front mapped out in front of you, peppered with symbols, polarizes opinion: for some, it clarifies everything they must do; for others, it is a baffling and chaotic representation. Whichever camp you fall into, it makes sense to learn how they work because you are bound to encounter them as you develop your skills. In their simplest form, charts are used to illustrate a repeat of a stitch pattern. They may be only a few stitches across, and a few rows in depth. For most people this is easy to work with, and this is where we will begin.

In a chart one square represents one stitch, therefore each line represents one row. On many charts the squares will not be shown absolutely square—you may recall in the last workshop we discussed the fact that stitches are not square but rectangular (see page 90). Some charts reflect this but others do not. Ideally there will be numbers up the side of the chart, representing the rows, and along the bottom, representing the stitches. When reading a chart, begin at the bottom right-hand corner and read across to the left for your first row, which should always be a right-side row. Wrong-side rows are read from left to right.

Below is an example of a very simple chart, representing a knit and purl design on the right side of the knitting. The knit stitches are shown by an empty square and the purl stitches have a dash across them. Everywhere you see a purl symbol you should purl the stitch on a right-side row, but knit it on a wrong-side row.

> ### Keeping track
>
> Before beginning to work with any type of complex chart make a photocopy of it, so you can scribble any notes on it and cross off each row as you work it. If you put your knitting down for the evening and resume work the following day it is all too easy to forget where you are in a chart and work the wrong row. Pulling back highly patterned work can be very dispiriting, so do take this precaution—it will help you avoid such calamity.

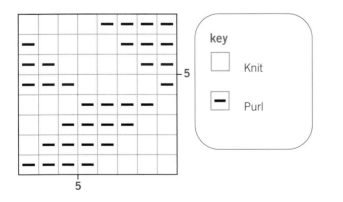

Unfortunately there is not a standard symbol lexicon for charts, so although it is common that a dash represents a purl stitch, it is not universal—some charts might use a dot instead, for example. What *will* always be present, however, is a key to the symbols employed in that particular chart, or within that book. Make sure you familiarize yourself with the symbols in the key before you begin, to avoid mistakes.

Other types of chart

Charts are almost always used to show color work patterns. Not only is this much briefer in terms of words, it is also very helpful to be able to see the finished pattern and compare how it should look to your own work as it develops. We will look more extensively at color work charts in Workshops 16 and 17 (see pages 136–137 and 146–148).

Charts are also often used to show the patterns in beaded knitting, because again it is very helpful to be able to see a visual representation of the actual design. Workshop 18 contains a beaded project that uses a chart within its instructions (see page 156).

Charts and cables

Instructions for cable patterns can be written in longhand, or shown in chart form. All-over cable patterns, and more complex repeats, tend to have a chart because it can be terribly lengthy to write out all the separate moves. It is also easy to lose your way in such long instructions. Cable-pattern charts will show the stitches traveling via a set of lines. Initially it is useful to be able to view and understand how the cables fit together, but when you come to use the charts you need to separate out each pair of lines row by row and treat each pair in isolation as an individual move to be worked.

Understanding cable symbols

Although there is no universally accepted set of symbols, there is a very common code when charting cables. A pair of lines will run from the starting point to the end point for each group of stitches involved in a cable, and will show whether the cable crosses to the left or to the right. The width between the two lines will be the same number of squares as there are stitches.

Here is a set of the most common symbols:

Cable symbols

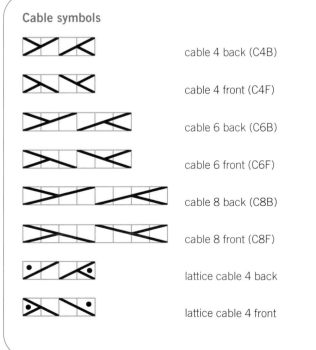

	cable 4 back (C4B)
	cable 4 front (C4F)
	cable 6 back (C6B)
	cable 6 front (C6F)
	cable 8 back (C8B)
	cable 8 front (C8F)
	lattice cable 4 back
	lattice cable 4 front

Cable sample chart

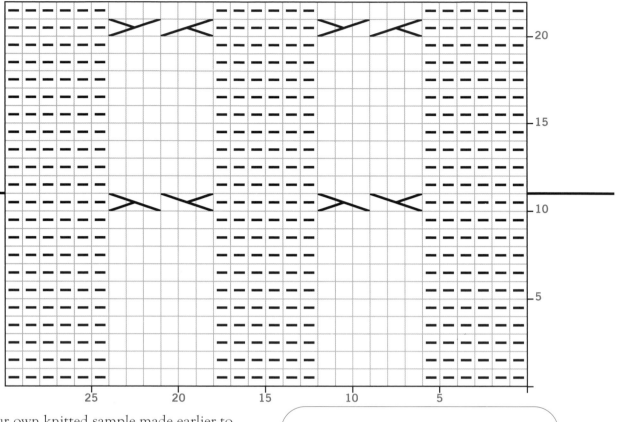

Compare your own knitted sample made earlier to the chart given here and familiarize yourself with the language and symbols. The horizontal line extending at each side of the chart shows where the cables changed direction.

If you made your own further cable samples, as suggested, try and apply the symbol methodology to the samples you made and create charts to match.

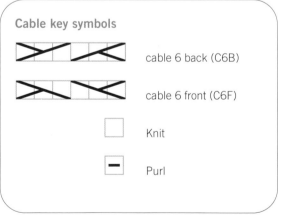

Cable key symbols

cable 6 back (C6B)

cable 6 front (C6F)

Knit

Purl

Cable abbreviations

When written out in longhand, cables are commonly abbreviated as "C," followed by the number of stitches across the whole cable (our examples above would therefore be a 6), followed by F, if it is a front cable, and B, if a back cable. So, our initial cables were two sets of C6F followed by two sets of C6B.

Cables that are worked over 4 stitches will be C4F or C4B; those worked over 10 stitches will be C10F or C10B and so on.

The Messenger Bag project that follows uses a range of simple cables, repeated in a regular sequence so that you can really get to grips with the technique. Cabling skills will be further developed in the Funnel Neck Sweater project that follows Workshop 12 (see page 112).

Messenger bag

A gloriously chunky, generous-size bag, made up of simple pieces, with a separate strap and lining. Although there are a lot of cables they occur in a regular sequence so the pattern is easy to grasp. This is the perfect project to practice cabling.

techniques used

Cabling in front

Cabling in back

Mattress stitch

Backstitch

yarn

Debbie Bliss Rialto Chunky (100% wool) chunky (bulky) yarn

10 x 1¾ oz (50 g) balls—656 yd (600 m)—of shade 010 Duck Egg

needles

One pair of US size 8 (5 mm) needles

other materials

Cable needle

Blunt darning needle

1.1 yd (1 m) of cotton ticking lining fabric

Sewing machine (optional)

Two large snap fasteners

Sharp sewing needle and thread to match main yarn

finished measurements

17 in. (43 cm) wide x 11 in. (28 cm) deep

gauge (tension)

16 sts and 22 rows to 4 in. (10 cm) working cable pattern using US size 8 (5 mm) needles.

abbreviations

g st	garter stitch
k	knit
C4F	cable 4 in front
C4B	cable 4 in back
C6F	cable 6 in front
C6B	cable 6 in back
k	knit
p	purl
patt	pattern
rep	repeat
rev st st	reverse stockinette (stocking) stitch
RS	right side
st st	stockinette (stocking) stitch
st(s)	stitch(es)
WS	wrong side

To make the messenger bag

Cast on 72 sts.

Work 6 rows in g st.

Begin cable patt 1:

Row 1: K4, p2, k4, p2, k12, p2, k4, p2, k8, p2, k4, p2, k12, p2, k4, p2, k4.

Row 2: K6, p4, k2, p12, k2, p4, k2, p8, k2, p4, k2, p12, k2, p4, k6.

Row 3: Rep Row 1.

Row 4: Rep Row 2.

Row 5 (cable row): K4, p2, C4F, p2, C6F, C6B, p2, C4B, p2, C4B, C4F, p2, C4F, p2, C6F, C6B, p2, C4B, p2, k4.

Row 6: Rep Row 2.

Row 7: Rep Row 1.

Row 8: Rep Row 2.

This 8-row sequence forms patt rep for bag front. Work a further 6 reps of cable patt 1 sequence.

Begin cable patt 2:

(In this second patt the edge g st panel is replaced by rev st st.)

Judging the strap length

Choose how long to make the strap by pinning it in place then trying the bag over your shoulder—you can wear it either over the shoulder or across the body diagonally. If it needs to be shorter, move the strap further down the side panel; if it needs to be a little longer, then move the strap further up the side panel. For our bag the strap is attached all the way down the side panels.

When happy with the position, use a length of knitting yarn in the needle and backstitch the strap in place to create a firm, strong seam. Repeat at the other side of the bag.

Row 1: P6, k4, p2, k12, p2, k4, p2, k8, p2, k4, p2, k12, p2, k4, p6.

Row 2: K6, p4, k2, p12, k2, p4, k2, p8, k2, p4, k2, p12, k2, p4, k6.

Row 3: Rep Row 1.

Row 4: Rep Row 2.

Row 5 (cable row): P6, C4F, p2, C6F, C6B, p2, C4B, p2, C4B, C4F, p2, C4F, p2, C6F, C6B, p2, C4B, p6.

Row 6: Rep Row 2.

Row 7: Rep Row 1.

Row 8: Rep Row 2.

Work a further 5 reps of cable patt 2 sequence.

Base section:

Work 12 rows of g st.

Work 6 reps of cable patt 2 sequence.

Work 6 rows in g st.

Bind (cast) off.

Side panels

(make 2 alike)

Cast on 9 sts. Work in g st until work measures 10 in. (25 cm).

Bind (cast) off.

Strap

Cast on 12 sts.

Row 1: K2, p2, k4, p2, k2.

Row 2: K4, p4, k4.

Rows 3 and 5: Rep Row 1.

Rows 4, 6, and 8: Rep Row 2.

Row 7: K2, p2, C4F, p2, k2.

Rep this 8-row sequence 36 times, then rep Rows 1–6 once again.

Bind (cast) off.

Making up

Weave in all loose tails and block all pieces. Pin the bottom of a side panel to the base section on one side of the main piece. With a length of the main yarn in the darning needle and working mattress stitch with RS facing, join the side panel to the main piece starting where the first cable patt sequence meets the second (where the garter stitch edge stops). Work down the length of the side panel to the bottom, sew along the base section to join the bottom of the side panel to the base section, then work up the last edge of the side panel ending at the end of the last garter stitch horizontal edge.

Rep for the other side panel. Weave in all loose tails.

Reinforce strap:
Cut a piece of lining fabric 3 in. (7.5 cm) wide and to match with the length of the strap. If your fabric is not long enough to accommodate this in one piece, cut two pieces each 1 in. (2.5 cm) longer than half the strap length and sew them together with a 1 in. (2.5 cm) seam allowance, trying to align any design so that the seam is not noticeable. Iron the fabric strip. With WS facing pin a ⅜ in. (1 cm) hem along each long edge. Stitch in place, preferably on a sewing machine. Pin the strap lining to the WS of the knitted strap piece, and handstitch in place using a very small straight stitch, so that it barely shows—it should cover the back of the cabled area, leaving some of the garter stitch edges free.

Attach the strap:
Pin the ends of the strap to the side panels of the bag, with RS facing.

Bag lining

To make the lining, cut the lining fabric to a width of 17 in. (43 cm) and a depth of 20½ in. (52 cm). With RS together, fold in half horizontally and pin the side seams with a ⅜ in. (1 cm) seam allowance.

Fold a ⅜ in. (1 cm) hem to the outside around the top edge of the lining fabric and sew in place.

Finishing

Securely stitch one half of a snap fastener onto each corner of the front flap and the other halves onto the front of the bag in a matching position.

Lightly steam press the strap flat.

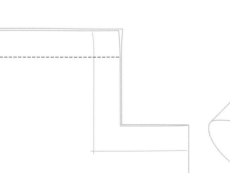

1 At the fold line measure up from the fold and in from the side by 1 in. (2.5 cm) and mark and then cut a square into the corners. Mark a ⅜ in. (1 cm) seam allowance along the sides of the square. Sew along the side seams and then press the seams open.

2 Open out a corner and refold so the side seam aligns over the bottom fold line and the cut edges meet in a horizontal line. Sew along the horizontal seam with a ⅜ in. (1 cm) seam allowance. Repeat for the other corner.

Place the lining inside the bag and stitch in place around the edge, across the flap and to the strap lining, using small straight stitches. You can also catch the lining to the bag at the bottom corners inside, although this is not essential.

Workshop 12

Making a garment

You now have most of the skills needed to knit a garment, but there is one technique we have not covered yet—knitting in rounds, rather than rows. This workshop allows you to practice this technique, and we will also look at how to match up shapings when working a neckline. Finally, we cover raglan and fully-fashioned shaping methods. The project in this workshop, a Funnel Neck Sweater, uses knitting in the round to work the neckline and also develops further skills in cabling to create the patterned panel.

Knitting in the round

All the knitting we have produced so far has been accomplished by knitting back and forth in rows, known as flat knitting. However, you can also work a piece in continuous rounds and this method is

used to create necks, socks, tubular pieces such as skirts, and often entire sweaters. For some people, it is by far their preferred method: it avoids the need to work any rows on the wrong side because the right side is always facing you, and in stockinette (stocking) stitch you will always be working knit stitches. Complicated color work patterns are worked more easily in the round because you can always see the right side of the work. In some cultures, knitting in the round has been the norm for centuries, and is a much older technique than the familiar flat knitting. Styles of knitting have developed to reflect this: for instance, the patterned sweater designs of Icelandic origin.

When knitting in the round it is essential to keep track of where you start each round: if you do not know where you began, you will not know when you have reached the end of a round. This is usually achieved through the use of markers: these are ring-shaped and fit loosely on the needles, sitting between the first and last stitch without interfering with the quality of the knitting.

Being able to make use of flat and circular knitting when each seems the best approach for a given situation makes for a very confident knitter. It is entirely appropriate to work the body of a heavy sweater on flat needles and in separate pieces, then switch to a circular needle to work the neckline and collar. Our Funnel Neck Sweater uses this approach.

Equipment

To knit in the round, you need to use a different type of knitting needle altogether. There are two options, the more common being a circular needle, which consists of two needle ends attached to a flexible nylon cord. The stitches are worked on the needle tips, then slid onto the cord. As the cord fills up, the stitches are pushed along to the tip of the left needle again, to be worked once more in the next round.

Circular needles are available in all the regular knitting needle sizes, and with varying lengths of cord. You might think, on first reflection, that it would be best to go for the longest available circular needle so that you are ready for any size project that you might choose to undertake. This is not so; if you use a circular needle that is too long for your knitting you will constantly have to slide the stitches along the cord so they will become very stretched and distorted. So in fact it is better use a circular needle that is slightly shorter than the circumference

Features of knitting in the round

A distinguishing feature of circular knitting is that there is a slight step or "jog" between rounds. Generally speaking, it is best to try and begin the rounds in a place where this is less likely to be noticeable, if possible.

Knitting in the round avoids the need to sew up many seams.

Garments worked entirely in the round become very heavy, are less portable to work on, and are much harder to pull back should you make a mistake.

of the knitting. Circular needles begin at a length of approximately 12 in. (30 cm) and go up to 40 in. (100 cm) and beyond. Very small circles should be knitted with double-pointed needles (dpns) instead.

Stitches required by size of circular needle

Gauge (tension) (no of stitches to)	Minimum–maximum number of stitches to fit needle length							
1 in. (2.5cm)	4 in. (10 cm)	16 in. (40 cm)	20 in. (50 cm)	24 in. (60 cm)	28 in. (70 cm)	32 in. (80 cm)	40 in. (100 cm)	48 in. (120 cm)
3–6	12–18	54—102	66–126	78–150	90–174	102–198	126–246	150–294
3½–7	14–28	62–118	76–146	90–174	104–202	118–230	146–286	174–342
4–8	16–32	70–134	86–166	102–198	118–230	134–262	166–326	198–390
4½–9	18–36	78–150	96–186	114–222	132–258	150–294	186–366	222–438
5–10	20–40	86–166	106–206	126–246	146–286	166–326	206–406	246–486
5½–11	22–44	94–182	116–226	138–270	160–314	182–358	226–446	270–534
6–12	24–48	102–198	126–246	150–294	174–342	198–390	246–486	294–582
6½–13	26–52	110–214	136–266	162–318	188–370	214–422	266–526	318–630
7–14	28—56	118–230	146–286	174–342	202–398	230–454	286–566	342–678
7½–15	30–60	126–246	156–306	186–366	226–426	246–486	306–606	366–726
8–16	32–64	134–262	166–236	198–390	230–454	262–518	326–646	390–774
8½–17	34–68	142–278	176–346	210–414	244–482	278–550	346–686	414–822
9–18	36–72	150–294	186–366	222–438	258–510	294–582	366–726	438–870

Incidentally, circular needles can also be used on flat knitting as if they were straight needles, going back and forth rather than round and round. You will, of course, then have to also work wrong-side rows as you would if using straight needles. But when working very large flat pieces of knitting, circular needles offer a much longer length to amass stitches onto than conventional straight pairs of needles.

Knitting in the round on a circular needle

First, make sure you have the right size needle (see chart on page 107). Cast on to one of the tips, sliding the stitches off onto the nylon cord as you go along, until you have the required number of stitches. Spread the stitches out along the length of the cord and tips evenly.

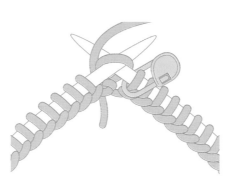

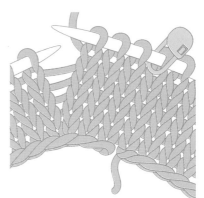

1 Make sure all the stitches are facing the same way: check that the bases of the stitches are all sitting at the bottom all round. If they are not, twist them around until they are all sitting the same way. This is really important: if you do not check this carefully and a twist becomes knitted into your fabric from the first row onward, you will not be able to put it right without unraveling it all.

2 Now bring the ends of the circular needle together in front of you, so that the start of your cast-on row is at the tip of your left needle, and the end of it is at the tip of the right one. Keep the stitches all facing the right way, then place your stitch marker on the right needle and push it along so that it sits in front of the stitches. Insert the tip of the right needle into the first stitch on the left needle and begin the first round.

3 You can now keep knitting in the usual way, and you should notice that your knitting is joined in a circle. When you reach the stitch marker you have reached the end of the first round, so slip your stitch marker onto the right needle again, then begin Round 2.

Changing from straight needles to a circular within a garment

If you need to make a neckline or collar within a garment, you will often make the pieces of the body on straight needles, then use a circular needle for the neck. In order to make this switch, you may have to knit stitches that have been stored on a holder, or pick up along bound (cast) off edges, using the circular needle. Again, a key point is to make sure that all the stitches you pick up are facing the same way, with their bases at the bottom. If you are picking up stitches from several flat pieces of knitting, to become one long round, then it is important that you start and finish the whole picking-up/casting-on exercise in one sitting to avoid any possibility of accidentally twisting the stitches after you have set your work down temporarily.

Picking up stitches

For more detailed information on picking up stitches see Workshop 10, Picking up stitches, pages 88–91, and to remind yourself how to work with held stitches, consult Workshop 9, Holding stitches, pages 81–82. The difference in this situation is that you might have to do both things at the same time, within one long round. This is why using a circular needle, with its capacity to hold more stitches, is a perfect solution for knitting neat necklines and collars.

In the sweater project in this workshop you will pick up stitches from edges and held stitches. As with most patterns, the right length of circular needle to use is given in the equipment list.

Fully fashioning

In Workshop 6 we mentioned the term "fully fashioning," which means working increases and decreases in the 2nd, 3rd, or 4th stitch in from the edge of the knitting. In very fine knits it might be even further in from the edge. In commercially-produced knitwear it is the mark of a better quality piece, because it is a more expensive way to achieve shaping. In hand knitting it is just as straightforward as shaping at the edge of a piece, but looks far more professional.

Fully fashioning is most frequently used around armholes and sleeves. In the photograph (right) you can see there is a defined band of knit stitches that follow a diagonal where the shaping occurs. This band is where the shaping has taken place.

The following sweater project has fully fashioned decreases, so the following exercise is a chance to practice these before you undertake the garment.

Paired increases and decreases

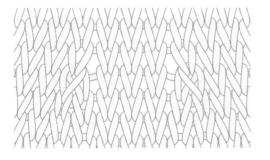

In Workshop 6 we learned how different ways of decreasing stitches will push the work in different directions (see Directional shaping, pages 61–64), so it is possible to decrease to the right, to the left or, in the case of a double decrease, both at the same time. Increasing stitches tend not to have such a defined and obvious slant, so it is less important to choose a particular method to use when increasing.

When working decreases or increases for some parts of a garment you must work them in pairs, teaming a right slanting decrease with a left slanting decrease at opposite edges of the garment, so that they match up symmetrically on the piece. This can happen when working the sleeve, back, or—in the case of a sweater—the front.

Paired decrease practice
Before beginning the sweater project that follows try working this sample, so that you feel confident to work perfect fully fashioned paired decreases in your garment.

Special abbreviations:
k2tog: insert right needle into front of next 2 sts, from left to right, then knit them together as if they were 1 st (see page 61)
ssk: slip 1 stitch knitwise twice, then insert left needle into front of these 2 sts and knit them together (see page 63)

Cast on 30 sts and work 4 rows in garter stitch, then 6 rows in stockinette (stocking) stitch, ending with a purl row.
Decrease row: K2, ssk, k to last 4 sts, k2tog, k2.
Work 10 more rows, then work the decrease row again.
You will notice that the decreases are following a defined line, and the little Vs mimic the diagonal line of the decreased edge—you have just created fully fashioned, paired decreases.

Shaping at the neckline

Knitting pattern designs for garments often have a back piece that is made without any sort of indented neckline shaping. The piece is made straight as far as the armholes and then, if these are present (and they may not be in very boxy shaped knits), they are decreased and shaped in pairs as described on page 109. The piece is then made straight right up to the shoulders and bound (cast) off. There may be minimal shaping of a neckline, with stitches bound (cast) off at each shoulder and the central groups bound (cast) off last, to form part of the neckline.

The main shaping for a neckline will happen in the front of a garment. The bottom part and the armholes will be knitted to match the back, and then a little farther up the pattern you may see the phrase "divide for neck." This will be the point at which your neckline shaping will begin.

Make a neat transition

Wherever possible, slip the center group of stitches that will form the lower "dip" of the neckline onto a stitch holder, rather than binding (casting) them off, especially when working the front neck. Your garment will look far neater if you do so, because the front neck will then flow seamlessly into the collar or neckline itself. Binding (casting) off adds a seam that will be more noticeable in an area that receives a lot of attention, directly below the face.

Similarly if you can hold the stitches at the sleeve tops when working raglan sleeves, rather than binding (casting) them off, then you can make a neat transition into the neckline here too.

Arm yourself with a good collection of stitch holders so that you are always equipped to take this option where possible. The project that follows uses this method.

Commonly, you will be asked to work one side of the neck before the other. The stitches not in use will be held on a stitch holder until the first side is complete. You might even find that you are asked to work two sequences of shaping at the same time—one that continues the armhole shaping and one that forms the neckline. This can be complicated and does require a degree of concentration. On the plus side, such areas tend to be relatively short so you will not have to do this for long. The pattern instruction will often specify "at the neck edge" for decreases that need to be worked here, to help you remember where you are in the piece.

Neckline shaping often follows the following type of sequence: binding (casting) off a few stitches at the neck edge, then decreasing one stitch every row a few times, then every other row for a few rows, then larger gaps between decreases, such as four or six rows. The decreases will follow the intended slant of the neckline in terms of their direction. This will sometimes be given in the instructions for the first side of the neckline, but if it is not refer to what you already learned above and in Workshop 6 (see Directional shaping, pages 61–64).

When working the right-hand side of the neckline, and working with the RS facing, your neckline decreases would need to slope to the right. At the armhole, they would slope to the left. At the left-hand side of the neckline, your neckline decreases would need to slope to the left, while your armhole decreases would slope to the right.

Work to match other side of neck

Often knitting patterns abbreviate what you need to do by using the phrase "Work to match other side of neck." If you look at Shaping at the neckline, opposite, this will be easy to work out, even though it sounds like a vague direction. Here is an example:

Divide for neck: K21, turn.
Left neck edge next row: Bind (cast) off 2 sts at neck edge, k to end.
Dec 1 st at neck edge on each of foll 4 rows, then dec 1 st at neck edge on every other row 3 times.
Knit 6 rows without shaping.
Bind (cast) off.

You have been working the left neck edge, working decreases that slope to the left (ssk or sl 1, k1, psso). Then the instructions say:

Rejoin yarn, bind (cast) off center 40 sts, then k to end. Work right side of neck to match left side, reversing all shapings.

The first problem is that you bound (cast) off 2 stitches at the left-hand neck edge on the first row, but you will reach the right neck edge at the end of the purl row, and you cannot bind (cast) off at the end of a row. So you should band (cast) off 3 stitches at the start of the following knit row—this will combine both the bound (cast) off 2 stitches, and the

Changing the look

If you want to give the neckline a fully-fashioned appearance, you can work the decreases on the 2nd or 3rd stitch in from the neck edge, rather than the edge stitch. This technique is particularly effective when working a V-neckline, where a sharper, defined look adds to the appeal.

If you used the fully fashioning technique on the first side, make sure that you also use it when working the second side so they will match perfectly.

decrease 1 stitch required at the start of the next row. Then decrease 1 stitch at the neck edge on only the following 3 rows, to allow for the one already done. Since decreases on the right side of the neck need to slant to the right use k2tog instead of the decrease method used for the left side, but otherwise work the same sequence as you did for the left side.

The Funnel Neck Sweater pattern asks you to match shapings in this way, but now you will be able to work out which decrease method to use when.

Raglan shaping

This is a type of garment shaping with gentle, evenly-spaced, sloping decreases that begin at the armholes and run up the front, back, and sleeves, all following the same path. The sleeves are long at the top and end at the neck itself, forming the shoulders in a soft slope. The sleeve raglans are sewn to the raglans on the front and back, then the top of each piece is picked up to form the neckline.

Here are diagrams of a raglan sweater (1), a conventionally shaped, inset sleeve sweater (2), and a drop-shoulder sweater (3). Note the differences in the shapes. Now that you have a good grip on shaping, you might begin to work out how these are achieved. Garments in subsequent workshops will discuss these further.

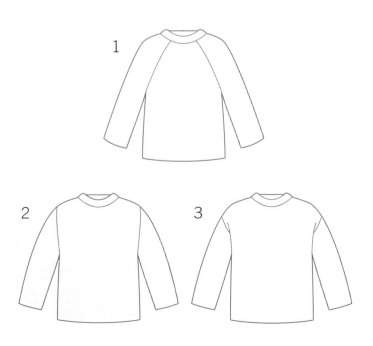

Funnel neck sweater

This snuggly, boxy sweater has raglan shaping and a central cabled panel. The neck is worked using a circular needle and the chunky yarn means the knitting grows quickly.

techniques used

Cable in front

Cable in back

Holding stitches

Picking up stitches

Working in the round

yarn

Cascade 128 (100% wool) yarn

7(**8**:9) x 3½ oz (100 g) hanks—128 yd (117 m) per hank—in shade 1952 Blaze

needles

Pair of straight US size 10 (6 mm) needles

Pair of straight US size 10½ (6.5 mm) needles

Circular US size 10 (6 mm) needle, 16 in. (40 cm) long

other materials

Cable needle

Blunt darning needle

4 stitch holders

size

To fit US size

4–6	8–10	12–14

To fit UK size

8–10	12–14	16–18

actual measurements

Bust

in.	42	42½	49
cm	107	116	125

Length to back neck

in.	23	24	25
cm	58	61	63.5

gauge (tension)

13 sts and 19 rows to 4 in. (10 cm) working stockinette (stocking) stitch using US size 10½ (6.5 mm) needles.

abbreviations

alt	alternate
beg	beginning
cont	continu(e)ing
C3B	slip next st on cable needle and hold at back of work, k next 2 sts off left needle, then p st off cable needle
C3F	slip next 2 sts onto cable needle and hold at front of work, p next st off left needle, then k next 2 sts off cable needle.
C4B	slip next 2 sts onto cable needle and hold at back of work, k next 2 sts off left needle, then k next 2 sts off cable needle
C4F	slip next 2 sts onto cable needle and hold at front of work, k next 2 sts off left needle, then k next 2 sts off cable needle.
foll	follow(s)ing
inc 1	increase 1 stitch by knitting twice into next st
k	knit
k2tog	knit 2 stitches together
p	purl
patt	pattern
sl	slip
sl 1, k1, psso	slip 1, knit 1, pass slipped stitch over
st(s)	stitch(es)
st st	stockinette (stocking stitch)
rem	remain(ing)
rep	repeat
RS	right side
WS	wrong side

To make the sweater

Back

Using US size 10 (6 mm) straight needles cast on 74(**80**:86) sts.

Work 4 rows in k1, p1 ribbing.

Change to US size 10½ (6.5 mm) straight needles.**

Work in st st, beg with a k row.

Work straight with no shaping until piece measures 14½(**15½**:16) in./37(**39**:40.5) cm, ending with RS facing for next row.

Shape armholes:

Bind (cast) off 4 sts at beg each of next 2 rows.

Begin raglan shaping:

*Next row: K2, sl 1, k1, psso, k to last 4 sts, k2tog, k2.

Next row: P to end.

Rep from * until 28(**32**:36) sts rem, ending on a p row.

Cut yarn and sl rem sts onto st holder.

Front

Work as for Back to **.

Begin cable patt:

Row 1: K23(**26**:29), p2, k4, p6, k4, p6, k4, p2, k23(**26**:29).

Row 2: P23(**26**:29), k2, p4, k6, p4, k6, p4, k2, p23(**26**:29).

Row 3: K23(**26**:29), p2, K4, p5, C3B, C3F, p5, k4, p2, k23(**26**:29).

Row 4: P23(**26**:29), k2, p4, k5, p2, k2, p2, k5, p4, k2, p23(**26**:29).

Row 5: K23(**26**:29), p2, C4F, p4, C3B, p2, C3F, p4, C4B, p2, k23(**26**:29).

Row 6: P23(**26**:29), k2, p4, k4, p2, k4, p2, k4, p4, k2, p23(**26**:29).

Row 7: K23(**26**:29), p2, k4, p3, C3B, p4, C3F, p3, k4, p2, k23(**26**:29).

Row 8: P23(**26**:29), k2, p4, k3, p2, k6, p2, k3, p4, k2, p23(**26**:29).

Row 9: K23(**26**:29), p2, C4B, p2, C3B, p6, C3F, p2, C4F, p2, k23(**26**:29).

Row 10: P23(**26**:29), k2, p4, k2, p2, k8, p2, k2, p4, k2, p23(**26**:29).

Row 11: K23(**26**:29), p2, k4, p2, k2, p8, k2, p2, k4, p2, k23(**26**:29).

Row 12: Rep Row 10.

Row 13: K23(**26**:29), p2, C4F, p2, C3F, p6, C3B, p2, C4B, p2, k23(**26**:29).

Row 14: Rep Row 8.

Row 15: K23(**26**:29), p2, k4, p3, C3F, p4, C3B, p3, k4, p2, k23(**26**:29).

Row 16: Rep Row 6.

Row 17: K23(**26**:29), p2, C4B, p4, C3F, p2, C3B, p4, C4F, p2, k23(**26**:29).

Row 18: Rep Row 4.

Row 19: K23(**26**:29), p2, k4, p5, C3F, C3B, p5, k4, p2, k23(**26**:29).

Row 20: Rep Row 2.

Row 21: K23(**26**:29), p2, C4F, p6, C4F, p6, C4B, p2, k23(**26**:29).

Row 22: Rep Row 2.

Row 23: Rep Row 3.

Row 24: Rep Row 4.

Row 25: K23(**26**:29), p2, C4B, p4, C3B, p2, C3F, p4, C4F, p2, k23(**26**:29).

Row 26: Rep Row 6.

Row 27: Rep Row 7.

Row 28: Rep Row 8.

Row 29: K23(**26**:29), p2, C4F, p2, C3B, p6, C3F, p2, C4B, p2, k23(**26**:29).

Row 30: Rep Row 10.
Row 31: Rep Row 11.
Row 32: Rep Row 12.
Row 33: K23(**26**:29), p2, C4B, p2, C3F, p6, C3B, p2, C4F, p2, k23(**26**:29).
Row 34: Rep Row 14.
Row 35: Rep Row 15.
Row 36: Rep Row 16.
Row 37: K23(**26**:29), p2, C4F, p4, C3F, p2, C3B, p4, C4B, p2, k23(**26**:29).
Row 38: Rep Row 18.
Row 39: Rep Row 19.
Row 40: Rep Row 20.
Row 41: K23(**26**:29), p2, C4B, p6, C4F, p6, C4F, p2, k23(**26**:29).
Row 42: Rep Row 22.
Rows 3 to 42 form cable patt sequence.
Work in cable patt as set, without shaping, until work measures 14½(**15½**:16) in./37(**39**:40.5) cm, ending with RS facing for next row.
Shape armholes:
Work as for Back, cont to work cable patt as set over central panel of sts, and working st st either side.
Begin raglan shaping:
*****Next row:** K2, sl 1, k1, psso, work in patt to last 4 sts, k2tog, k2.
Next row: Patt to end.
Rep from * until 36(**40**:44) sts rem, ending on a WS row.
Divide for neck:
Next row: K2, sl 1, k1, psso, k4, turn,
Shape neck:
Next row: P3, p2tog, p2.
Next row: K2, sl 1, k1, psso, k2.
Next row: P1, p2tog, p2.
Next row: K2, sl 1, k1, psso.
Next row: P1, p2tog.
Next row: K2tog.
Fasten off.
Slip center 20(**24**:28) sts onto st holder. Rejoin yarn to next st on left needle.
Shape neck to match left side:
Next row: K4, k2tog, k2.
Next row: P2, p2tog, p3.
Next row: K2, k2tog, k2.
Next row: P2, p2tog, p1.
Next row: K2tog, k2.
Next row: P2tog, p1.
Next row: K2tog, fasten off.

Sleeves
(both alike)
Using US size 10 (6 mm) straight needles, cast on 34(**36**:38) sts.
Work 10 rows in k2, p2 ribbing.

Shape sleeve as foll:
Change to US size 10½ (6.5 mm) straight needles. ***Work 6 rows in st st without shaping, beg with a k row,
Next row: K2, inc 1 in next st, k to last 3 sts, inc 1 in next st, k2.
Next row: P to end.
Rep from *** until you have 54(**56**:58) sts, then work straight without shaping until sleeve measures 20 in. (51 cm).
Begin raglan shaping:
Next row: K2, sl 1, k1, psso, k to last 4 sts, k2tog, k2.
Next row: P to end.
Cont working in st st and shaping raglan every other row in this way, until 14 sts rem, sl these sts onto st holder.

Finishing
Weave in all loose yarn tails. Block pieces.

Collar
Using circular US size 10 (6 mm) needle and with RS facing, slip sts off Back st holder onto circular needle, then sts off left Sleeve st holder. Pick up and k 4 sts down left side of neck, then slip center sts off Front st holder onto circular needle. Pick up and k 4 sts up right side of neck, then sl sts off right Sleeve st holder onto circular needle. Place st marker to show start of round. Working in st st (k all sts, because you are working in the round rather than back and forth in rows), k straight for 20 rounds.
Next round: [P2, k2] to end of round.
Rep this last round another 3 times.
Bind (cast) off loosely in rib.

Making up
Weave in loose yarn tails from neck. With RS facing, and using darning needle and a length of yarn, join all raglan seams, joining the front to each sleeve first, then the back, using mattress stitch. Next join side seams, again using mattress stitch, before finally joining the sleeve seams using mattress stitch.

TIP
To wear, either roll the neck down, or keep it standing up for warmth.

How to turn a heel

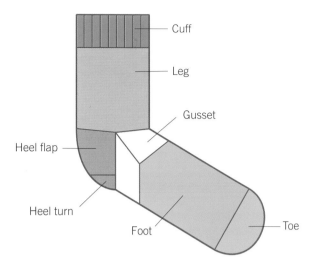

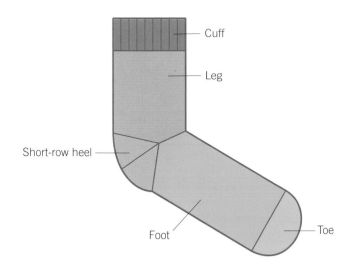

Turning the heel of a sock is a skill that divides opinion. The traditional way involves creating two separate elements: the heel flap and the actual turned heel. The former is a section that is worked back and forth and may be worked in a thicker yarn or with two strands, so that it is reinforced. The heel flap is worked on only a section of the stitches; the others remain in a held position. After the heel flap is completed, a smaller heel is turned on the same stitches; the terminology refers to changing the direction of the knitting so that the foot lies at a 90° angle to the leg part. Turning the heel involves decreasing this group of stitches at either side so that a small central group of stitches is then joined to the held stitches, to continue as the instep and foot section.

The heel flap is the part of the sock that must withstand the most wear and tear, so for traditional boot socks, or for men's socks, this should be the method used. Should you wish to learn this more complex method, see the reading list on page 171 for some good sources. However, for our pattern we are going to learn a more modern-day, simplified version of the heel turn that is perfectly suitable for socks that are going to experience lighter, everyday use. It involves making a one-piece heel created through the use of the short rowing technique and holding stitches.

Working a one-piece heel

To practice this, use the sample you made earlier for Working shapings in the round. For this method, first you must divide the number of stitches you have after working the leg by two. Imagine you have just worked the leg of the sock and are about to turn the heel. You have 30 stitches in your sample, so you will need 15 for the heel.

Slip a total of 15 stitches onto one dpn, then slip the remaining 15 stitches onto a stitch holder. These stitches will remain held until we need them again to knit the foot part

of the practice sock. Put two of the empty dpns aside for the moment.

Now work in rows rather than rounds, using only two dpns as you would a pair of straight needles. Knit 14 sts, then bring the yarn round the needle to wrap the next stitch, and slip it purlwise onto the right needle, turn.

Next row: Slip wrapped st onto right needle, p13, yarn round needle to wrap last st, slip it onto right needle, turn.

Next row: Slip wrapped st onto right needle, k12, wrap next st, slip onto right needle, turn.

Next row: Slip wrapped st onto right needle, p11, wrap next st, slip, turn.

Next row: Slip wrapped st onto right needle, k10, wrap next st, slip, turn.

Next row: Slip wrapped st onto right needle, p9, wrap next st, slip, turn.

You have now worked half the turned heel. From this point on you will build the stitches back up again before the turn is complete.

Next row: Slip first wrapped st, k across 8 sts to next wrapped st, lift wrap onto left needle and knit tog with next st, wrap next st, turn.

Next row: Slip first wrapped st, p9 to next wrapped st, lift wrap onto left needle and p tog with next st, wrap next st, turn.
Next row: Slip first wrapped st, k10, lift wrap and k tog with next st, wrap next st, turn.
Next row: Slip first wrapped st, p11, lift wrap and p tog with next st, wrap next st, turn.
Next row: Slip first wrapped st, k12, lift wrap and k tog with next st, wrap next st, turn.
Next row: Slip first wrapped st, p13, lift wrap and p tog with next st, wrap next st, turn.
Next row: Slip first wrapped st, k to end of row.

Now redistribute your stitches over the three dpns as before, taking care to avoid any twisting, and making sure they are evenly spread. Work a further 3 rows in stockinette (stocking) stitch—this is the start of the "foot" section of this practice sock. You should be able to see that you have created a section that projects outward from the main knitting, and looks like a little heel.

In the following project, Simple Slouchy Socks, you will use this same method over a larger number of stitches, using finer yarn than we have so far worked with.

A note about sock yarn

It may be tempting to work socks up in the softest yarns and indeed, for slouching socks that are intended for use indoors without shoes, this is completely acceptable. However, for socks that will endure normal everyday wear and tear it is much better to use a special sock yarn. These yarns are spun more tightly and often have a small amount of nylon content, both of which considerably increase their durability.

Sock yarn tends to be quite fine, because it is intended for the knitting of regular-thickness socks that will fit into shoes. It is available in plain colors, but also comes in a range of dyed effects. Some are hand painted in random stripes, like the yarn we have used for the Simple Slouchy Socks (see page 120); others are printed in a sequence of measured lengths of interchanging colors, which produce a neat, striped pattern when they are knitted up. Because the color changes are carefully worked out by the yarn dyer, the resultant socks will look as though the knitter has changed color repeatedly throughout the knitting, when in fact the yarn has done all the work. This type of yarn is known as self-striping.

For the sock project overleaf, you might want to seek out some special sock yarn and try out some of the effects available.

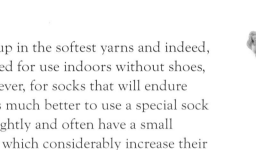

Simple slouchy socks

Here is a pair of comfortable, cozy socks slightly shaped in the leg with a turned heel, worked up in hand-painted sock yarn. Although the yarn and needles are very fine they are straightforward to use, so by the time you have finished you should be a whizz with double-pointed needles.

techniques used

Using double-pointed needles

Turning a heel

Wrapping stitches

Slipping stitches

yarn

Cascade Heritage Paints (75% Superwash wool/25% nylon) yarn

1 x 3½ oz (100 g) skein—437 yd (399.5 m)—of shade 9903 Sage Honey

needles

Set of five US size 1–2 (2.5 mm) double-pointed needles

other materials

Stitch marker

Stitch holder

Blunt darning needle

size

To fit average female feet, sizes

US 6–7 (**8–9**)

UK 4–5 (**6–7**)

gauge (tension)

33 sts and 40 rows to 4 in. (10 cm) working stockinette (stocking) stitch using US size 1–2 (2.5 mm) needles.

abbreviations

cont	continue
dec	decrease
dpn	double pointed needles
k	knit
k2tog	knit 2 stitches together
p	purl
rem	remainder
rep	repeat
sl	slip
st(s)	stitch(es)
st st	stockinette (stocking) stitch
tog	together

To make the socks
(make 2 the same)
Leg section:
Cast on 74(**80**) sts onto one dpn. Sl 26(**28**) sts onto a second dpn then sl next 24(**26**) sts onto a third dpn. Arrange dpns so that all sts face the same way, and are not twisted. Make sure st bases all face in toward center of triangle. Place st marker by last cast-on st to mark start of round.
Round 1: Using fourth dpn as working needle, k first st of row, pulling last cast-on st close to avoid a noticeable join (see page 117). P next st and work rem of round in k1, p1 rib. At end of round, move st marker up before moving to next round.
Round 2: [k1, p1] to end. Move marker up (rep at end of every round from here onward).
Work a further 6 rounds in rib as set. (8 rounds)
Work 56(**62**) rounds straight in st st (knit all sts when working in the round).
Next round (dec round): K7, k2tog, [k13(**14**), k2tog] to last 5(**7**) sts, k5(**7**). 69(**75**) sts
Work 6 rounds straight in st st.
Next round (dec round): K6, k2tog, [k12(**13**), k2tog] to last 5(**7**) sts, k5(**7**). 64(**70**) sts
Work 6 rounds straight in st st.

Turn heel:
Sl 6(**7**) sts onto first dpn, keep next 32(**35**) sts on second dpn, sl rem sts onto st holder (including those on the first dpn). 32(**35**) sts
Working with just 2 dpns as if they were straight needles, work in rows as follows:
Row 1: K31(**34**), bring yarn forward to wrap next st, then sl it purlwise onto right dpn, turn.
Row 2: Sl wrapped st onto right dpn, p30(**33**), wrap last st, sl onto right dpn, turn.
Row 3: Sl wrapped st onto right dpn, k29(**32**), wrap next st, sl, turn.
Row 4: Sl wrapped st onto right dpn, p28(**31**), wrap next st, sl, turn.
Row 5: Sl wrapped st onto right dpn, k27(**30**), wrap next st, sl, turn
Cont in this way, wrapping last st and always slipping as indicated, until you have worked central group of 16(**19**) sts (halfway point of the heel).
Row 17: Sl first wrapped st, k across to next wrapped st, lift wrap onto left dpn and k it tog with wrapped st, wrap next st, turn.
Row 18: Sl first wrapped st, p across to next wrapped st, lift wrap onto left dpn and p it tog with wrapped st, wrap next st, turn.
Rep these two rows until all wrapped sts have been worked. 32(**35**) sts on right needle
Foot:
Rearrange sts back over four dpns, using spare dpn to help slip them off st holder in right direction if necessary. Make very sure to place st marker at start of round, in same position as before—this is essential to help place toe in right position later.
Work 50(**62**) rows straight in st st.
Toe:
Round 1: K2tog, k27(**30**), k2tog, k1, k2tog, k27(**30**), k2tog, k1.
Round 2: K to end.
Round 3: K2tog, k25(**28**), k2tog, k1, k2tog, k25(**28**), k2tog, k1.
Round 4: K to end.
Round 5: K2tog, k23(**26**), k2tog, k1, k2tog, k23(**26**), k2tog, k1.
Round 6: K to end.
Round 7: K2tog, k21(**24**), k2tog, k1, k2tog, k21(**24**), k2tog, k1.

Round 8: K to end.
Round 9: K2tog, k19(**22**), k2tog, k1, k2tog, k19(**22**), k2tog, k1.
Round 10: K to end.
Round 11: K2tog, k17(**20**), k2tog, k1, k2tog, k17(**20**), k2tog, k1.
Round 12: K to end.
Bind (cast) off rem sts.

Finishing

Join toe seam using mattress stitch (see Workshop 5, page 55). Weave in all loose tails. Check heel section for any holes or loose stitches; this can happen when switching from working in rounds to working in rows, and vice versa. Use a short length of yarn to sew any holes closed, making as few stitches as possible but drawing the threads closed neatly.

Press the socks lightly under a damp dish towel.

Workshop 14

Bobbles, fringing, and edges

We have spent some time focused on the creation of garment pieces over the last couple of workshops. As a contrast, this workshop shows you how to make raised textures through working different variations on bobbles, and also looks at some other decorative texture effects. Finally, it covers how to make a fringe and some other types of edging. The project after this workshop, a textured throw, is constructed in individual squares that are then joined together and finished off with a fringed edge.

Bobbles

In Workshop 11 we learned how to make cables (see pages 97–99). In traditional Aran patterns these are often used in conjunction with bobbles to create deep texture effects. Bobbles can also be used alone as a textured pattern, and when worked in a contrast color they offer a very dramatic effect. They are a little fiddly to work, but after mastering the technique it is simply a matter of repetition.

Working a bobble
A bobble is created by increasing several times into the same stitch, then decreasing in the following row.

By increasing just once into a stitch, then decreasing in the following row, you will create a tiny indent of texture. Increasing more than once into the same stitch produces a larger physical area for the bobble. You can widen the increased area to include two or more stitches, and/or work several rows of short rowing over the increased stitches, before decreasing, which will create a defined ridge or bobble.

As with cables, the definition of the bobble pattern increases when a knit bobble is worked on a purl background, so bobbles are often worked on a reverse stockinette (stocking) stitch background. The following samples produce three variations of a bobble, each of which creates a slightly different raised textural effect.

Simple bobble
This produces a standard bobble that is quite raised for visual impact.

Special stitch:
MB (Make Bobble)
[yon, k1] 3 times in next st, turn, sl 1 st, p5, turn, sl 1 st, k5, turn, p2tog 3 times, turn, sl 1 st, k2tog, psso

Cast on 30 sts.
Rows 1 and 3 (RS): K to end.
Rows 2, 4, and 6: P to end.
Row 5: [K5, MB] to end of row.
These 6 rows form patt.
Work 2 more rows in stockinette (stocking) stitch.

Examine the bobbles you have made. You will notice that there might be a slight gap in the knitting between the edges of the bobbles and the main knitting in between them: this is quite normal and does not usually cause any problems on the densely patterned fabrics that bobbles tend to occur on. However, if you are working your bobbles in very thick yarn and on very large needles, you may opt to sew some small basting (tacking) stitches after the piece is finished, to join these gaps up a little so that they don't show so much.

Flattened bobbles
A variation on the above technique, this produces more coin-like discs of pattern that do not have the same raised impact as a regular bobble.

Work 5 rows in stockinette (stocking) stitch, ending on a knit row.
Next row: P5, *[k1, yo, k1] into same stitch, p4; rep from * to end of row, turn.
Next row: [K4, p3] to last 5 sts, k5, turn.
Next row: P5, [k3, p4] to end, turn.
Next row: [K4, p3tog] to last 5 sts, k5, turn.
Work 2 more rows in stockinette (stocking) stitch.

Compare the textures to the bobbles you made earlier—you will notice that they are less pronounced and lie flatter within their background. This texture is a useful one to combine with cable patterns in lighter weight sweaters, when a thick bobble texture would be too heavy for the garment.

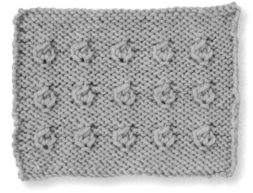

Little bobbles
This pattern is created all over the same row, and involves making many increases into the same stitch.

Special stitch:
Make bobble (MB): [K1, p1, k1, p1, k1, p1, k1] all into front of next st without slipping it off left needle until end of sequence, then lift the 2nd, 3rd, 4th, 5th, 6th, and 7th loops over the first stitch on right needle, one at a time. (one bobble made)

Work 5 rows in stockinette (stocking) stitch, ending on a purl row.
Bobble row: P2, (MB, p1) to end of row.
Work 2 more rows in stockinette (stocking) stitch.

Look at the last textures made—you will see that there is no gap between the edges of the bobbles and the main fabric because the increase and decrease were made in the same row, so no extra height was created. This texture is very appealing; because of its smaller scale, it is suitable for use in baby or children's items.

Loops and fringes

Fringing can be applied as an edging, or you can make a loopy fabric that is slow to knit but has a lovely retro appeal. There are a few variations on the techniques below, but all produce a similar effect.

Loop knitting
To create a loopy fabric some dexterity is required, but once you have got used to looping the yarn around your thumb the rest is easy.

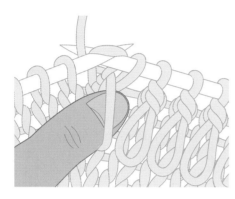

Cast on 25 sts.
Work 4 rows in garter stitch (see Workshop 1, page 24).
Next row: K1, *pick up loop between last and next st with left needle as if for a M1 increase, then slip it purlwise onto right needle. Bring yarn forward and wrap around your thumb clockwise before taking to the back again. Keeping the wrapped loop around the thumb, slip the picked-up loop from right needle to left needle, then knit

together with next st (k2tog). Release your thumb from the wrapped loop, which should be secure. Repeat from * to end of row.
Next row: K to end, tightening loops by pulling gently on each to secure firmly. Repeat these two rows another 4 times.

This method works best with a thick, fluffy yarn. You can adjust the length of the loops by changing the position of your thumb: the lower down the piece you hold it, the longer the resulting loops.

Fringed edging
There are a few ways to create a fringe, but the below is a tried and tested method.

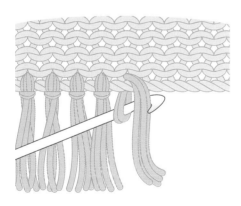

You will need a medium to large size crochet hook to complete this edging. Attach the fringing to the bottom edge of your bobble sample.

Wrap the yarn around a small book eight times, then cut the end. Cut through the loops at one end so that you have eight short lengths of yarn. Fold two strands in half and insert a crochet hook into the loop to pull it through one stitch of the bottom edge of the

knitted sample. Grab the ends with the hook of the crochet hook and pull them through the loops as shown. Pull to tighten.

Repeat these steps to add the remaining tassels of the fringe. You can place the tassels as close together or as far apart as you wish, and increase or reduce the number of strands of yarn in each to create thicker or finer fringing.

Alternative edging methods

You can knit edgings as separate pieces that are added after the main body of the work is complete, or you can incorporate them into the knitting as you go along. Separately constructed edgings can be produced either horizontally or vertically, which opens up additional options for short rowing flounces and frills created using a similar method as for the Short-row Wrap in Workshop 8 (see page 77).

Certain types of projects benefit from an edging knitted vertically, because there would be too many stitches to work them horizontally. Afghans, bedcovers, and shawls are all easier to finish off with a vertical edging. Smaller projects such as pillows, sweaters, and table covers can be edged from either orientation. The following samples are examples of edgings made horizontally and vertically, so you can practice both techniques.

Horizontal edging: pointed edge

This edging can be made to whatever length required, but on a long piece you would need to keep some of the points on stitch holders because the needles would eventually become too crowded to work effectively.

Cast on 2 sts.
Row 1: K2.
Row 2: Yo, k2.
Row 3: Yo, k3.
Row 4: Yo, k4.
Row 5: Yo, k5.
Row 6: Yo, k6.
Row 7: Yo, k7.
Row 8: Yo, k8.
Row 9: Yo, k9.
Row 10: Yo, k10.
Row 11: Yo, k11.
Row 12: Yo, k12.
Row 13: Yo, k13.
Row 14: Yo, k14.

One point completed. Break yarn and push point to far end of needle. Cast on another 2 sts and work a second point in exactly the same way, then repeat for a third point, but do not break the yarn at the end of knitting the third point.

Next row: Turn, k across all sts on needle to join points together.
Next row: K all sts.
Work another 4 rows all knit.
Bind (cast) off.

Vertical edging: diamond lace

Many fancy edges are created using lace techniques, which we look at in more detail in the next workshop, but here is a straightforward pattern that employs familiar stitches to create a diamond filigree pattern. To recap how to knit three stitches together, see Workshop 6 page 63.

Cast on 10 sts.
Row 1 and every alt row: K.
Row 2: K4, k2tog, yo, k2tog, [yo, k1] twice.
Row 4: K3, [k2tog, yo] twice, k3, yo, k1.
Row 6: K2, [k2tog, yo] twice, k5, yo, k1.
Row 8: K4, [yo, k2tog] twice, k1, k2tog, yo, k2tog.
Row 10: K5, yo, k2tog, yo, k3tog, yo, k2tog.
Row 12: K6, yo, k3tog, yo, k2tog.
Repeat this sequence of rows another 2 or 3 times, then bind (cast) off.

When working vertical edges, you can simply keep knitting until you have produced the desired length. If you find that the pattern looks better if you complete a repeat before finishing, then do so even if the result is a little too long—you can always put this right with a little creative blocking (see page 26).

The Squares Throw that follows is constructed by making a set of squares, each employing some textural techniques, which are then joined and finished with a fringe. You will have the chance to practice the techniques in this workshop and revise your cabling skills again. The next workshop will look at lace knitting in more detail, building on the foundations laid in Workshop 8 and through the above edging sample.

Squares throw

This luxurious throw, designed by Pauline Richards, is soft to snuggle into or can be sized up for a bed by knitting more squares. The squares are joined patchwork style to create a richly textured design edged with a knotted fringe.

techniques used

Cable cast on

Making bobbles

Cables

Combining textural stitches

Creating a fringed edge

Mattress stitch to join

yarn

Debbie Bliss Cashmerino Aran (55% extra-fine merino wool/33% microfiber/ 12% cashmere) worsted (Aran) yarn

16 x 1¾ oz (50 g) balls—1568 yd (1440 m)—in shade 102 Beige

needles

Pair of US size 8 (5 mm) needles

other materials

Cable needle

Blunt darning needle

Crochet hook

finished measurements

Each square: 12 in. (30 cm) square

Throw: 44 in. (110 cm) square, including fringe

gauge (tension)

18 sts and 24 rows to 4 in. (10 cm) working stockinette (stocking) stitch using US size 8 (5 mm) needles.

abbreviations

cont	continue
C4B	cable 4 back
C4F	cable 4 front
k	knit
k2tog	knit 2 stitches together
LH	left-hand
p	purl
p2tog	purl 2 stitches together
patt	pattern
psso	pass slipped stitch over
rep	repeat
RS	right side
sl	slip
st(s)	stitch(es)
WS	wrong side
yon	yarn over needle
[]	repeat sequence within square brackets the number of times indicated

special abbreviation

MB (Make Bobble)
[yon, k1] 3 times in next st, turn, sl 1 st, p5, turn, sl 1 st, k5, turn, [p2tog] 3 times, turn, sl 1 st, k2tog, psso.

To make the throw:
Knit 9 assorted squares, varying the number of each design as prefered—the aim is to create a patchwork effect.

Vertical bobble square
Using cable method, cast on 53 sts.
Rows 1 and 3 (RS): K to end.
Rows 2, 4 and 6: P to end.
Row 5: K5, [MB, k5] to end of row.
These 6 rows form patt.
Cont in patt until 81 rows have been completed.
Bind (cast) off.

Bobbles and cables square
Using the cable method cast on 53 sts.
Rows 1, 3, 5, and 7 (WS): K3, [p8, k5] 3 times, p8, k3.
Rows 2 and 6: P3, [k8, p5] 3 times, k8, p3.
Row 4: P3, [C4B, C4F, p5] 3 times, C4B, C4F, p3.

Row 8: P3, [k8, p2, MB, p2] 3 times, k8, p3.
These 8 rows form patt.
Cont in patt until 79 rows have been completed.
Row 80: Rep Row 2.
Row 81: Rep Row 1.
Bind (cast) off.

Bobble cluster and basket stitch square
Using cable method, cast on 53 sts.
Rows 1 and 3 (RS): [K3, p3] 4 times, k29.
Row 2: P29, [k3, p3], 4 times.
Rows 4 and 6: P26, k3, [p3, k3] 4 times.
Row 5: P3, [k3, p3] 4 times, k26.
Rep Rows 1–6 twice.
Row 19: [K3, p3] 4 times, k15, MB, k1, MB, k11.
Row 20: P29, [k3, p3] 4 times.
Row 21: [K3, p3] 4 times, k14, MB, k1, MB, k1, MB, k10.
Row 22: P26, [k3, p3] 4 times, k3.

Row 23: P3, [k3, p3] 4 times, k12, MB, k1, MB, k11.
Row 24: P26, [k3, p3] 4 times, k3.
Rep Rows 1–6 twice more, then Rows 1–3 once (39 rows worked in total).
Row 40: [K3, p3] 4 times, k5, [p3, k3] 4 times.
Row 41: [P3, k3] 4 times, p5, [k3, p3] 4 times.
Row 42: Rep Row 40.
Rows 43 and 45: K29, [p3, k3] 4 times.
Row 44: [P3, k3] 4 times, p29.
Rows 46 and 48: [K3, p3] 4 times, k3, p26.
Row 47: K26, [p3, k3] 4 times, p3.
Rep Rows 43–48 once, then Rows 43–46.
Row 59: K11, MB, k1, MB, k12, [p3, k3] 4 times, p3.
Row 60: Rep Row 46.
Row 61: K10, MB, k1, MB, k1, MB, k14, [p3, k3] 4 times.
Row 62: Rep Row 44.
Row 63: K11, MB, k1, MB, k15, [p3, k3] 4 times.
Row 64: Rep Row 46.
Row 65: Rep Row 47.
Row 66: Rep Row 48.
Rep Rows 43–48 twice, then Rows 43–45. (81 rows worked in total)
Bind (cast) off.

Finishing
Block squares or steam lightly without pressing down to avoid flattening the bobbles.

Making up
Lay out squares and sew together using mattress stitch (see page 55.
Make fringe (see page 124) using a book 5¼ in. (13 cm) wide to wrap the yarn around, with 4 strands for each tassel. Place tassels evenly around all sides of throw. Trim fringe to neaten.

Joining and aftercare

When joining a vertical edge to a horizontal edge using mattress stitch, sew approximately 2 rows to every stitch, but use your judgment to ensure an even seam. Pin before you sew, to help maintain a neat join.

You can arrange the squares in your own pattern, but if you alternate the direction of the knitting on each square it will give a more even shape and tension across the throw.

Hand wash or machine wash as wool.

Working lace patterns

Now we have developed skills in textural patterning and cables, it is time to move on to another aspect of more advanced knitting: using yarn overs and decreases to produce delicate, lacy, openwork fabrics. Lace fabrics grow quickly, use less yarn than solid fabrics, and are practical for summer because the decorative holes offer ventilation. In this workshop we use yarn overs creatively to make simple eyelet designs, faggoting, and complex lace. We then look at how to work shapings in a lace pattern. There are samples for you to practice before you move on to a stylish Lace Shell Top project.

Revising yarn overs

In Workshop 8 we learned that a yarn over (or yarn forward) can work as a basic increase, but also creates a decorative hole (see page 76). To exploit the decorative hole effect without adding to the number of stitches on the needle, you must work a decrease to counteract the increase made.

Working the yarn over before a k2tog decrease will angle the work very slightly to the right.

Working a [sl 1, k1, psso] decrease after the yarn over will tip the work very slightly to the left.

In the Short-row Wrap project (see page 77), we alternated this sequence to maintain straight edges because, although the slant is very tiny, a long series of them will have a more pronounced effect on the edge of the work.

Using an ssk or [sl 1, k1, psso] decrease also angles the path of the stitches more toward the left and a k2tog angles the path toward the right (see Workshop 6, pages 63 and 61). Many lace patterns exploit the ability to play with direction in this way by using different decreases or by changing the order of the yarn over/decrease.

Eyelet patterns

The simplest form of open work, an eyelet pattern, is defined as one where the eyelets have at least three rows of knitting between them vertically. The pattern may call for eyelets to be worked on every other row, but in true eyelet patterns they will not occur directly above one another any closer than three rows apart. They may be directly next to each other horizontally or can be spaced apart. Eyelets are also useful for creating tiny buttonholes or for threading ribbon or cord through to create a fastening. They are often seen in baby garments or vintage-style fitted short-sleeve tops.

Simple diamond eyelet pattern

Cast on 31 stitches and work 4 rows in garter stitch (see page 24). This pattern has a variation on the yo/decrease, because on some rows it uses a double decrease and a second yo to compensate for the extra increase made. It is a familiar design that was often worked into knitted undergarments in the past.

Pattern row 1: K to end.
Row 2 and every alt row: P to end.
Row 3: K3, *yo, ssk, k6; rep from * to last 4 sts, yo, ssk, k2.
Row 5: K2, *yo, sl 1, k2tog, psso, yo, k5; rep from * to last 5 sts, yo, sl 1, k2tog, psso, yo, k2.
Row 7: Rep Row 3.
Row 9: K to end.
Row 11: Rep Row 9.
Row 13: K7, *yo, ssk, k6; rep from * to end.
Row 15: K6, *yo, sl 1, k2tog, psso, k6; rep from * to last st, k1.
Row 17: Rep Row 13.
Row 18: P to end.

Repeat this 18-row sequence one more time, then examine your work; you will see the center of the diamond shape, where the double decrease was worked, and where the [ssk] decreases have tipped the stitch path toward the left. There are clear knitted boundaries between the eyelets in this pattern, and they maintain their rounded appearance because of this. Next we look at what happens when eyelets are worked in close succession and lose their rounded definition. Work 4 rows in stockinette (stocking) stitch, to separate out the samples.

Chevron faggoting

This second pattern is more open and you may notice a change in the width of the swatch as a result. Because the eyelets are worked in close succession they appear more square and look like ladders when grouped together. These ladder patterns are known as faggots, because they imitate the faggoted embroidered seams fashionable in the 16th century.

Row 1: K1, *[yo, ssk] twice, k1, [k2tog, yo] twice, k1; rep from * to end.
Row 2: P to end.
Row 3: K2, *yo, ssk, yo, sl 1, k2tog, psso, yo, k2tog, yo, k3; rep from * to last 9 sts, yo, ssk, yo, sl 1, k2tog, psso, yo, k2tog, yo, k2.
Row 4: P to end.
Rep this 4-row sequence another four times, remembering to work everything inside the square brackets as many times as specified before moving on to the next step.

You will have noticed that this sample grew quite quickly and seems a little wider than the previous one. As this pattern has many holes it also uses far less yarn, so the fabric is a lot lighter. Note the different appearance of the individual eyelets in the first sample and the groups in this second sample. Also note the pronounced direction of the ladders: faggoted patterns often feature diagonal lines of holes like this, and the direction of these can be emphasized by the type of decrease chosen (see page 128).

More complex lace

Lace knitting is a very old form of knitting, often used to produce treasured heirloom pieces. For example, traditional wedding ring shawls from the Shetland Islands are worked in extremely fine wool, on super-thin needles, with intricate designs. They are prized for their fineness—theoretically they can be drawn through a wedding ring despite their generous size.

Complex lace often has sections of eyelets as well as faggots, and will feature changes in direction and to the pattern instructions. It is probably the most technically difficult type of knitting to master and requires some patience, concentration, and skill. However, there are no stitches within it that you have not now learned, so you are ready to attempt such patterns when you wish!

Charts in lace work

We have seen how charts are used in knit and purl patterns and in cabling, so you are familiar with how they work. A different set of symbols is used to denote the stitches used in lace knitting—the example below shows how the eyelet pattern (see page 129) would be represented in chart form.

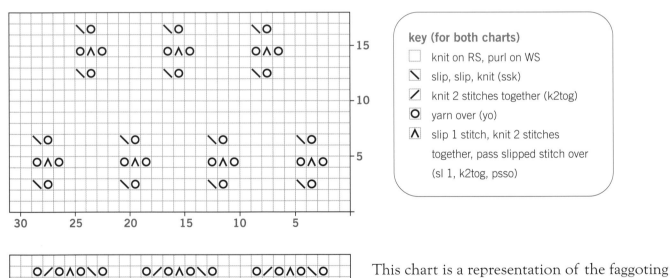

key (for both charts)

	knit on RS, purl on WS
╲	slip, slip, knit (ssk)
╱	knit 2 stitches together (k2tog)
O	yarn over (yo)
ʌ	slip 1 stitch, knit 2 stitches together, pass slipped stitch over (sl 1, k2tog, psso)

This chart is a representation of the faggoting sample (see page 129).

Compare both these charts to your samples and see if you can follow the stitches on the chart, noting where the yarn overs and decreases occur and the directions they take.

Keeping stitch numbers correct

The best way to check as you go along is to count your stitches after every row, to make sure you have the number you should have at that point in the pattern. If your pattern offers vague instructions, such as "dec one st each end of every other row 6 times," then you may find it helps to write out how many stitches you should have for each row, and check it off as you go along.

Shaping and openwork knitting

Openwork patterns are tricky when shaping, because you must use your judgment unless the pattern offers specific guidance, row by row. For example, instructions may just state "dec 1 st each end of next 8 rows." In stockinette (stocking) stitch this would be straightforward, because you simply k2tog, ssk, or [sl 1, k1, psso] on the second or third stitch from each edge. However, in a lace pattern where this is followed by a yo, you may find you have just replaced the decreased stitch just worked, and reversed it. The key is always to think of the yo

and decrease together as one unit, and where you do not have enough stitches to work both, work them in stockinette (stocking) stitch instead. This is where using your own judgment comes into play—each pattern will have a different point at which it becomes feasible to draw the stitches that have been increased at the edges into the lace pattern. Until then, just work them in stockinette (stocking) stitch. Many patterns provide charts to show you exactly where to work your increases and decreases—an example is shown below.

Practicing shaping in lace patterning

So that you can competently work the shaping that is required in the following project, knit this small sample and follow it on the chart at the same time:

Cast on 25 sts and work 4 rows in plain stockinette (stocking) stitch, ending on a p row.
Row 1: K1, *yo, ssk, k7, k2tog, yo, k1; rep from * once again.
Row 2: P to end.
Row 3: k2tog (dec 1 st), *yo, ssk, k5, k2tog, yo**, k3; rep from * to **, k2.
Row 4: P to last 3 sts, p2tog, p1.
Row 5: K2tog, k4, k2tog, yo, k5, yo, ssk, k3, k2tog, yo, k3.
Row 6: Rep Row 4.
Row 7: K2tog, k1, k2tog, yo, k7, yo, ssk, k1, k2tog, yo, k4.
Row 8: P to end.
Row 9: Sl 1, k2tog, psso, yo, k9, yo, sl 1, k2tog, psso, yo, k5.
Row 10: Rep Row 8.
Row 11 (start of next lace patt rep): K2tog, k2, k2tog, yo, k1, yo, ssk, k7, k2tog, yo, k1.
Row 12: Rep Row 8.
Row 13: K2tog, k2tog, yo, k3, yo, ssk, k5, k2tog, yo, k2.
Row 14: Rep Row 8.
Row 15: K2tog, yo, k5, yo, ssk, k3, k2tog, yo, k3.
Row 16: Rep Row 8.
Row 17: K8, yo, ssk, k1, k2tog, yo, k4.
Row 18: Rep Row 8.
Row 19: K9, yo, sl 1, k2tog, psso, yo, k5.
Row 20: Rep Row 8.

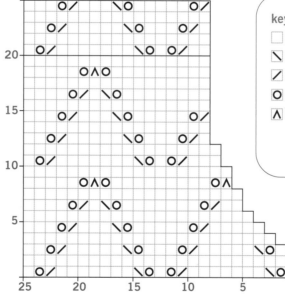

key
- ☐ knit on RS, purl on WS
- ◫ slip, slip, knit (ssk)
- ◪ knit 2 stitches together (k2tog)
- ◉ yarn over (yo)
- ◭ slip 1 stitch, knit 2 stitches together, pass slipped stitch over (sl 1, k2tog, psso)

Note: The horizontal line in the chart marks where the pattern continues straight once the shaping is completed.

Note how, on Rows 5, 7, and 17, you worked extra stockinette (stocking) stitches rather than patterning at the start of the shaping because there were insufficient stitches to accommodate both a yo and a decrease. On Row 15 the yo/dec could be worked even at the edge, because the two cancel each other out so did not result in a decrease. On Row 9, you could also work the patterning at the very edge because the pattern created two decreases in one stitch—one of these was compensated for by the yo, and the other

created a shaping decrease, which we wanted at this point in the armhole. Had it been higher up, where the knitting has no shaping, we would have had to work this differently and make just a single decrease paired with the yo, to avoid an unwanted loss of a stitch.

The project that follows is a sleeveless lace shell top, with shaping at the armholes and neckline. It has similar eyelets and decreases, and the shaping is detailed for each size.

Lace shell top

This pretty summer top is worked up in lightweight cotton. The armholes and front neckline have lace pattern repeats that adjust to the shaping, and at the back a single glass button forms an elegant fastening.

techniques used

Eyelets and lace

Holding stitches

Picking up stitches

Shaping in lace pattern

yarn

Rowan Cotton Glacé (100% cotton) yarn

5(6:6:7) x 1¾ oz (50 g) balls—125 yd (115 m) per ball—of shade 846 Cadmium

needles

Pair of straight US size 3 (3.25 mm) needles

Circular US size 3 (3.25 mm) needle

other materials

Blunt darning needle

Stitch holder

Glass button with shank base

size	1	2	3	4
To fit US size				
	4	6	8	10
To fit UK size				
	8	10	12	14

actual measurements

Bust				
in.	32½	35	36½	38
cm	85	89	93	97

Length				
in.	21¾	21¾	23½	23½
cm	55.5	55.5	59.5	59.5

gauge (tension)

20 sts and 31 rows to 4 in. (10 cm) working lace patt using US size 3 (3.25 mm) needles.

abbreviations

beg	beginning
cont	continue
dec	decrease
foll	follow(ing)
g st	garter stitch
k	knit
k2tog	knit 2 stitches together
LH	left-hand
p	purl
p2tog	purl 2 stitches together
patt	pattern
psso	pass slipped stitch over
rem	remain(ing)
rep(s)	repeat(s)
RS	right side
RH	right-hand
sl	slip
ssk	slip 1 stitch, slip 1 stitch, knit 2 stitches together
st(s)	stitch(es)
st st	stockinette (stocking) stitch
yo	yarn over

special note

Follow the correct instructions for the size being made. The lace pattern is the same for all, but the start point is different for each size, so at times instructions are divided in the pattern.

To make the top
Front
Cast on 85(89:93:97) sts.
Work 4 rows in g st.
Sizes 1(2) only begin lace patt:
Row 1: K4(6) *k2tog, yo, k1, yo, ssk, k7; rep from * to last 9(11) sts, k2tog, yo, k1, yo, ssk, k4(6).
Rows 2, 4, 6, and 8: P to end.
Row 3: K3(5) *k2tog, yo, k3, yo, ssk, k5; rep from * to last 10(12) sts, k2tog, yo, k3, yo, ssk, k3(5).
Row 5: K2(4), *k2tog, yo, k5, yo, ssk, k3; rep from * to last 11(13) sts, k2tog, yo, k5, yo, ssk, k2(4).
Row 7: K1(3), *k2tog, yo, k7, yo, ssk, k1; rep from * to last 0(2) sts, k0(2).

Row 9: K0(2), k2tog, yo, k9, *yo, sl 1, k2tog, psso, yo, k9; rep from * to last 2(4) sts, yo, ssk, k0(2).
Row 10: Rep Row 2.
Size 3 only begin lace patt:
Row 1: K8, *k2tog, yo, k1, yo, ssk, k7; rep from * to last 13 sts, k2tog, yo, k1, yo, ssk, k8.
Row 2: P to end.
Row 3: K7, *k2tog, yo, k3, yo, ssk, k5; rep from * to last 14 sts, k2tog, yo, k3, yo, ssk, k7.
Size 4 only begin lace patt:
Row 1: K1, yo, ssk, k7, *k2tog, yo, k1, yo, ssk, k7; rep from * to last 3 sts, k2tog, yo, k1.
Row 2: P to end.
Row 3: K2, yo, ssk, k5, *k2tog, yo, k3, yo, ssk, k5; rep from * to last 4 sts, k2tog, yo, k2.

Sizes 3(4) cont lace patt:

Rows 4, 6, 8, and 10: P to end.

Row 5: K1(**3**), yo, ssk, k3, *k2tog, yo, k5, yo, ssk, k3; rep from * to last 3(**5**) sts, k2tog, yo, k1(**3**).

Row 7: K2(**4**), yo, ssk, k1, *k2tog, yo, k7, yo, ssk, k1; rep from * to last 4(**6**) sts, k2tog, yo, k2(**4**).

Row 9: K3(**5**), *yo, sl 1, k2tog, psso, yo, k9; rep from * to last 6(**8**) sts, yo, sl 1, k2tog, psso, yo, k3(**5**).

All sizes:

These 10 rows form patt rep. Foll version that relates to your size until work measures 14½(**14½**:15¾:**15¾**) in./ 37(**37**:40:**40**) cm, and you have worked 11(**11**:12:**12**) reps of patt, ending with RS facing for next row. The foll sections are divided according to size, with instructions to adjust patt when shaping occurs.

Sizes 1(2) shape armholes:

Row 1: Bind (cast) off 6(**7**) sts , k next 0(**1**) st, *yo, ssk, k7, k2tog, yo, k1; rep from * to last 6(**8**) sts, yo, ssk, k4(**6**).

Row 2: Bind (cast) off 6(**7**) sts, p to end.

Row 3: K0(**1**), k2tog, *yo, ssk, k5, k2tog, yo, k3; rep from * to last 11(**12**) sts, yo, ssk, k5, k2tog, yo, k2tog, k0(**1**).

Row 4: P1, p2tog, p to last 3 sts, p2tog, p1.

Row 5: K2tog, k4(**0**), (size **2** only: yo, ssk, k3), *k2tog, yo, k5, yo, ssk, k3; rep from * to last 3(**4**) sts, (size 1 only: k1, k2tog), (size **2** only: k2tog, yo, k2tog).

Row 6: Rep Row 4.

Row 7: K2tog, k1(**2**), *k2tog, yo, k7, yo, ssk, k1; rep from * to last 2(**3**) sts, k0(**1**), k2tog.

Row 8: P to end.

Row 9: (Size 1 only: sl 1, k2tog, psso, yo), (size **2** only: k1, sl 1, k2tog, psso, yo), *k9, yo, sl 1, k2tog, psso, yo; rep from * to last 12(**13**) sts, k9, yo, sl 1, k2tog, psso, k0(**1**).

Row 10: Rep Row 8.

Row 11 (beg next lace patt rep): K2tog, k2(**3**), *k2tog, yo, k1, yo, ssk, k7; rep from * to last 9(**10**) sts, k2tog, yo, k1, yo, ssk, k2(**3**), k2tog.

Row 12: Rep Row 8.

Row 13: K2tog, k0(**1**), *k2tog, yo, k3, yo, ssk, k5; rep from * to last 9(**10**) sts, k2tog, yo, k3, yo, ssk, k0(**1**), k2tog.** Cont in patt as set, without further shaping until armhole measures 5½ in. (14 cm), ending with RS facing for next row.

Sizes 3(4) shape armholes:

Row 1: Bind (cast) off 7(**8**) sts, k next 0(**1**) st, *k2tog, yo, k1, yo, ssk, k7; rep from * to last 13(**15**) sts, k2tog, yo, k1, yo, ssk, k8(**10**).

Row 2: Bind (cast) off 7(**8**) sts, p to end.

Row 3: K2tog, k3(**4**), *yo, ssk, k5, k2tog, yo, k3; rep from * to last 2(**3**) sts, k0(**1**), k2tog.

Row 4: P1, p2tog, p to last 3 sts, p2tog, p1.

Row 5: K2tog, k2(**3**), *yo, ssk, k3, k2tog, yo, k5; rep from * to last 11(**12**) sts, yo, ssk, k3, k2tog, yo, k2(**3**), k2tog.

Row 6: Rep Row 4.

Row 7: K2tog, k1(**2**), *yo, ssk, k1, k2tog, yo, k7; rep from * to last 8(**9**) sts, yo, ssk, k1, k2tog, yo, k1(**2**), k2tog.

Row 8: Rep Row 4.

Row 9: K2(**3**), *yo, sl 1, k2tog, psso, yo, k9; rep from * to last 5(**6**) sts, yo, sl 1, k2tog, psso, yo, k2(**3**).

Row 10: Rep Row 4.

Row 11: K6(**7**), *k2tog, yo, k1, yo, ssk, k7; rep from * to last 11 sts(**to end**), k2tog, yo, k1, yo, ssk, k6.

Row 12: Rep Row 4.

Row 13: K4(**5**), *k2tog, yo, k1, yo, ssk, k5; rep from * to last 11 sts(**to end**), k2tog, yo, k1, yo, ssk, k4.

Row 14: Rep Row 4.

Row 15: K2(**3**), *k2tog, yo, k5, yo, ssk, k3; rep from * to last 11 sts(**to end**), k2tog, yo, k5, yo, ssk, k2.

Row 16: P to end.** Cont in patt as set, without further shaping, until armhole measures 6 in. (15 cm), ending with RS facing for next row.

All sizes shape front neck:

Keep working in patt.

Row 1: Patt 14(**15**:16:**17**) sts and turn, leaving rem sts on st holder.

Row 2: Dec 1 st at neck edge on each of next 6 rows. 8(**9**:10:**11**) sts

Work a further 7 rows without shaping.

Shape shoulder:

Bind (cast) off 4(**4**:5:**5**) sts at beg of next row.

Work 1 row.

Bind (cast) off rem 4(**5**:5:**6**) sts.

With RS facing, rejoin yarn to rem sts and bind (cast) off center 29 sts. Patt to end.

Complete to match first side, reversing all shapings.

Back

Work as Front to ** (end of armhole shaping).

Work straight without shaping until armhole measures 3 in. (7.5 cm), ending with RS facing for next row.

Divide for neck:

Patt 28(**24**:30:**31**) sts, turn, leaving rem sts on st holder.

From this point onward, work 4 sts at center neck edge in st st, not lace patt. Work patt across the other sts.

Right side of neck opening:
Work straight until Back measures 9 rows fewer than Front to start of shoulder shaping, ending with WS facing for next row.
Bind (cast) off 12 sts at beg of next row, then dec 1 st at neck edge on foll 8 rows, ending with RS facing for next row.

Shape shoulder:
Bind (cast) off 4(4:5:5) sts at beg of next row.
Work 1 row.
Bind (cast) off rem 4(5:5:6) sts.
With RS facing, rejoin yarn to rem sts and bind (cast) off first stitch. Patt to end (28:29:30:31 sts).
Work left side of neck opening to match right side, reversing all shaping.

Finishing
Weave in all loose tails.
Block pieces.
Using a length of yarn in darning needle, join shoulders using backstitch.

Back neck slit edgings:
With RS facing, pick up and knit 18 sts along one slit edge.
Work 3 rows in g st.
Bind (cast) off.
Rep for opposite side of back slit opening. Using a length of yarn in darning needle, stitch two edges together at base.

Neckband:
Using circular needle, with RS facing and starting at left side of back neck opening, pick up and knit 24 sts from left side of back neck opening, 12 sts down left side of front neck, 29 sts from center front, 12 sts up right side of front neck, and 24 sts across right side of back neck. Working in rows rather than rounds, work 2 rows in g st, then bind (cast) off.

Button loop:
Cast on 3 sts.
Knit 6 to 8 rows, depending on diameter of button.
Bind (cast) off and weave in loose tails.
Using a length of yarn in darning needle, form loop and sew at top RH edge of slit. Sew button in matching position on top LH edge of slit.

Armhole edgings:
With RS facing, pick up and knit 114(116:120:122) sts along one armhole edge.
Work 2 rows in g st.
Bind (cast) off.
Rep for other armhole.

Using a length of yarn in darning needle, join side seams using mattress stitch, and weave in all rem loose tails.

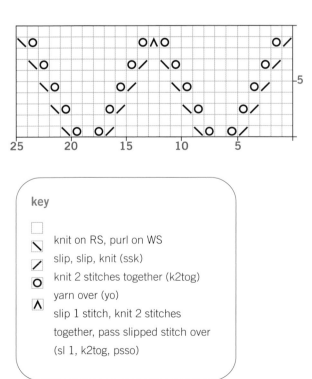

key

☐	knit on RS, purl on WS
╲	slip, slip, knit (ssk)
╱	knit 2 stitches together (k2tog)
O	yarn over (yo)
∧	slip 1 stitch, knit 2 stitches together, pass slipped stitch over (sl 1, k2tog, psso)

Color knitting using intarsia

Now you can work with extra needles and are familiar with checking your work, we can move on to working with several colors at a time using a technique called intarsia. We also look at another way to shape sleeves to match armholes, and see why certain methods of joining suit some situations better than others. The project for this workshop is a cute rabbit sweater for a child, perfect to practice with and bound to keep you smiling.

Charts and intarsia knitting

Using a chart for intarsia is incredibly helpful. Usually it will have colored squares representing the actual colors of yarn. So if you see 3 green squares next to 2 black squares, you know immediately to knit 3 stitches in green followed by 2 in black: it is an intuitive connection.

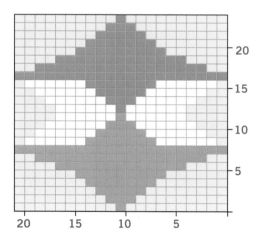

Working a chart

This chart is for an intarsia design: you can see that the rows and stitches are numbered, but the chart only shows the motif, not the whole sweater piece.

Typical instructions to position the chart would be:

Using A, k30(**32**:34:**36**), work Row 1 of chart to end;
using A k30(**32**:34:**36**).
Cont to work rem 23 rows of chart as set.

So for the *second* size, k32 in yarn A, then work the first row of the chart, reading from right to left, beginning in the bottom right-hand corner and changing color as appropriate. Join in a new balls of yarns B and A, work to the end of Row 1, then k32 in the second ball of yarn A to complete the row.

On the next row, p32 stitches plus the appropriate stitches in yarn A for Row 2 of the chart, reading from left to right. Change to yarn B where indicated, then back to the original ball of yarn A to complete Row 2, purling 32 stitches with that ball to finish.

Properties of intarsia

Intarsia is used to create large-scale color motifs, picture sweaters, or geometric designs and involves working with small balls of color and changing color within a row several times. The resulting fabric is only one layer thick (unlike Fair Isle or "stranded" knitting, which consists of the knitted fabric and a layer of threads at the back, see page 145).

Ga[...]

The[...]
hap[...]
garr[...]
shaj[...]
stru[...]
the [...]
dres[...]

Shaj
For a[...]
begu[...]
row ([...]
swea[...]
(cast[...]

Shaj
The [...]
repea[...]
and [...]
    Bir[...]
rows,[...]

M[...]

In r[...]
so a[...]
pro[...]

Bacl
Best [...]
lot of[...]
shou[...]
(see [...]
(see [...]
work[...]
drap[...]
or wl[...]
Back[...]
cloth[...]
tear.

Proportional graph paper

As noted earlier, knitted stitches are not square but rectangular, a little wider than they are long. This means charted patterns drawn up on normal graph paper will be disproportionate to the knitted results:

the knitted motif will look shorter and wider than the motif does on normal graph paper. The examples below show how the knitting actually looks when you follow a chart drawn out on normal graph paper.

Charts recap

We have not looked at charts in any detail since Workshop 11 (see page 100), so here is a quick recap.

- Charts are read from right to left on the right side
- Charts are read from left to right on the wrong side
- One square represents one stitch, one line represents one row
- Charts might show the entire garment, including shaping, or just show a repeat to work several times
- You usually begin at the bottom right-hand corner of a chart
- It is a good idea to make a photocopy of the chart—enlarged if possible—to cross out each row as you work it and annotate as needed

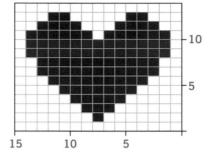

Here is a chart drawn on regular graph paper.

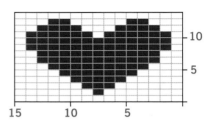

And here is what the knitting will look like if worked from this chart. The knitted motif is squatter, so rows need to be added to the chart to compensate.

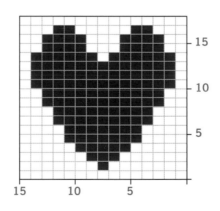

Here is the chart on regular graph paper, taking into account the extra rows needed.

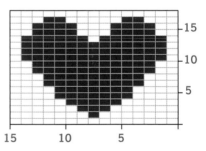

And here is what the knitting will look like if this new chart is followed.

Charts in knitting patterns are often constructed on regular, squared graph paper, so they may look distorted in comparison to the knitted results. If you want to design your own motifs, an alternative to working out how to adjust the proportions on regular graph paper is to use special knitter's graph

paper, known as proportional graph paper. This can be printed from several websites (see page 171) and you can draw freely on it to create your motif, safe in the knowledge that what you draw is what will be produced in knitting.

Rabbit sweater

This cute rabbit motif sweater has a large motif that allows you to practice following a chart and use the intarsia method of colorwork. The rest of the sweater is relatively plain, with inset sleeves and a ribbed crew neck. Choose any bright or pastel main color as your background.

techniques used

Colorwork using intarsia

Working with multiple balls of yarn

Following a chart

Holding stitches

Picking up and knitting stitches

Mattress stitch and back stitch seams

yarn

Debbie Bliss Rialto DK (100% wool) light worsted (DK) yarn

5(**5**:6) x 1¾ oz (50 g) balls—110 yd (100 m) per ball—of shade 060 Sky (A)

2(**2**:3) x 1¾ oz (50 g) balls—110 yd (100 m) per ball—of shade 060 Ecru (B)

1 x 1¾ oz (50 g) ball—110 yd (100 m)— of shade 060 Pink (C)

Oddment of Gray (D)

needles

Pair of US size 3 (3.25 mm) needles

Pair of US size 6 (4 mm) needles

other materials

2 x stitch holders

Blunt darning needle

size

To fit age

years	3-4	**5-6**	7-8

actual measurements

chest

in.	26½	**28¾**	30
cm	67	**73**	76

length

in.	15½	**16¼**	17
cm	39	**41**	43

sleeve length

in.	11½	**13¼**	15
cm	29	**34**	38

gauge (tension)

22 sts and 30 rows to 4 in. (10 cm) working stockinette (stocking) stitch using US size 6 (4 mm) needles.

abbreviations

alt	alternate
beg	beginning
cont	continue
dec	decrease
foll	follow(ing)
g st	garter stitch
k	knit
k2tog	knit 2 stitches together
p	purl
p2tog	purl 2 stitches together
p2tog tbl	purl 2 stitches together through back loops
psso	pass slipped stitch over
rem	remaining
rep	repeat
sl	slip
ssk	slip, slip, knit 2 stitches together
st(s)	stitch(es)
st st	stockinette (stocking) stitch
[]	repeat sequence within square brackets the number of times indicated

To make the sweater

Back

Using US size 3 (3.25 mm) needles and yarn A, cast on 74(**80**:84) sts.

Row 1: [K1, p1] to end.

Rep Row 1 another 7(**9**:9) times. 8(**10**:10) rows

Change to US size 6 (4 mm) needles.**

Starting with a k row, work in st st until work measures 10¾(**11**:11½) in./27(**28**:29) cm, ending on a p row.

Shape armholes:

Bind (cast) off 4 sts at beg of next 2 rows. 66(**72**:76) sts

Next row (dec row): K2, ssk, k to last 4 sts, k2tog, k2.

Work 1 row without shaping.

Rep last 2 rows 3 times more, then work dec row again. 56(**62**:66) sts

Work straight in st st until armholes measure 4¾(**5¼**:5½) in./ 12(**13**:14) cm, ending with a p row.

Shape shoulder:

Bind (cast) off 4(**5**:5) sts at beg of each of next 6 rows.

Slip rem 32(**32**:36) sts onto st holder.

Front

Work as for Back to **.

Starting with a k row, work 26(**26**:30) rows in st st without any shaping.

Using small amounts of yarn

Use a length of yarn for the areas of yarn D rather than wind a ball, because they are quite small.

Begin intarsia motif from chart.

Chart row 1: K24(**27**:29) sts in yarn A, then work Row 1 of chart over center 26 sts, then k24(**27**:29) sts in yarn A. This sets position of chart.

Work Rows 2–48 of chart, working st st in yarn A at either side.

Shape armholes:

Shape armholes as given for Back, AT THE SAME TIME cont to work chart.

Work straight for rem rows of chart, then work in st st using yarn A until 12 rows fewer than Back to start of shoulder shaping have been worked.

Shape neck:

Next row: K21(**24**:24) sts then turn, slipping rem sts onto st holder. Work each side of neck separately.

Dec row 1: P2, p2tog, p to end.

Dec row 2: K to last 4 sts, k2tog, k2.

Rep these 2 rows 3 times more.

Work 1 row without shaping.

Dec 1 st at neck edge on next row.

Work 1 row without shaping.

Shape shoulder:

Bind (cast) off 4(**5**:5) sts at beg of next and foll alt row.

Work 1 row without shaping.

Bind (cast) off rem sts.

With RS facing, keep center 14(**14**:18) sts on holder, then rejoin yarn to next st and k to end of row.

Dec row 1: P to last 4 sts, p2tog tbl, p2.

Dec row 2: K2, ssk, k to end.

Rep these 2 rows 3 times more.

Work 2 rows without shaping.

Dec 1 st at neck edge on next row.

Work 1 row without shaping.

Shape shoulder:

Bind (cast) off 4(**5**:5) sts at beg of next and foll alt row.

Work 1 row without shaping.

Bind (cast) off rem sts.

Sleeves

(make 2 alike)

Using US size 3 (3.25 mm) needles and yarn A cast on 42(**44**:46) sts.

Work 10 rows in k1, p1 rib.

Change to US size 6 (4 mm) needles, work 2 rows in st st with no shaping.

3rd size only:

Next row (inc row): K2, inc 1 in next st, k to last 3 sts, inc 1 in next st, k2. –(–:48) sts

Work 5 rows in yarn A without shaping.

All sizes:

Change to yarn B.

Work 2 rows in g st.

Next row: K2, inc 1 in next st, k to last 3 sts, inc 1 in next st, k2. 44(**46**:50) sts

Work a further 7 rows in st st without shaping, then rep inc row. 46(**48**:52) sts

Work 4 more rows in st st without shaping, then work 1 row all k.

Change to yarn A.

Work 2 rows in st st without shaping, then work inc row. 48(**50**:54) sts

Work 7 more rows in st st without shaping, then work inc row. 50(**52**:56) sts

Work 5 more rows in st st without shaping.

Change to yarn B.

Work 2 rows in g st, then work inc row. 52(**54**:58) sts

Work 7 rows in st st without shaping, then work inc row. 54(**56**:60) sts

Work a further 4 rows in st st without shaping, then work 1 row all k.

Change to yarn A.

Work 2 rows in st st without shaping, then work inc row. 56(**58**:62) sts

Work 7 rows without shaping then work inc row. 58(**60**:64) sts

Work 5 rows in st st without shaping.

Change to yarn B.
Work 2 rows in g st, then work inc row. 60(**62**:66) sts
Work 7 rows in st st without shaping, then work inc row.
62(**64**:68) sts
Work 4 rows in st st without shaping, then work 1 row all k.
Change to yarn A.
2nd and 3rd sizes only:
Work 2 rows in st st without shaping, then work inc row.
–(**66**:70) sts
Work 7 rows in st st without shaping, then work inc row.
–(**68**:72) sts
Work 5 rows in st st without shaping.
Change to yarn B.
3rd size only:
Work 2 rows in g st, then 4 rows in st st.
All sizes shape sleeve top:
Bind (cast) off 4 sts at beg of the next 2 rows. 54(**60**:64) sts
Next row (dec row): K2, sl 1, k1, psso, k to last 4 sts,
k2tog, k2.
Work 1 row without shaping, then work dec row again.
Rep these 2 rows twice more, then work dec row again.
Next row: P2, p2tog, p to last 4 sts, p2tog tbl, p2.
44(**50**:54) sts
Bind (cast) off rem sts.
Work second sleeve to match.

Finishing
Weave in all loose tails (see page 25). Block all pieces (see
page 26).
With yarn A in darning needle, join right shoulder seam
using backstitch (see page 33).
Collar:
Using US size 3 (3.25 mm) needles, yarn A and with RS of
work facing, pick up and k 12 sts down left side of front
neck, k center 14(**16**:18) sts off st holder, pick up and k
12 sts up right side of front neck, k 32(**32**:36) sts off st
holder at top of back. 70(**70**:78) sts
Work 8 rows in k1, p1 rib.
Bind (cast) off loosely in rib.

With yarn A in darning needle, join rem shoulder seam
using backstitch. Use mattress stitch (see page 55) to join
edges of collar. Weave in loose tails.
Pin one sleeve cap into one armhole and join using
backstitch. Rep with other sleeve cap. Join side and sleeve
seams using mattress stitch.
Weave in all rem loose tails.

Reading a chart

Remember to read the chart from right to left
on right-side rows, and from left to right on
wrong-side rows.

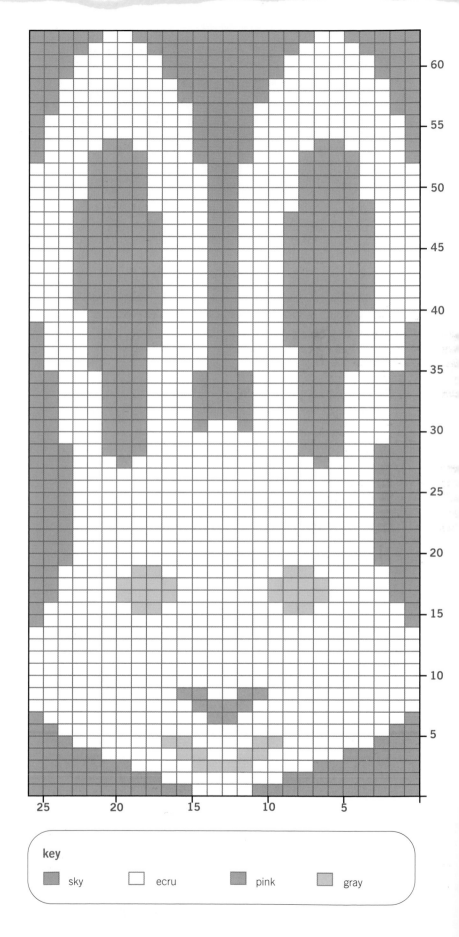

key

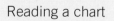 sky ⬜ ecru ⬛ pink ⬛ gray

Workshop 17

Color knitting with Fair Isle

In the second part of our focus on color knitting we will look at Fair Isle and how this differs from intarsia knitting. In this workshop you will learn how to manage working with many strands at the back of the work, and we will also return to the issue of charts and repeats. When your skills and knowledge of Fair-Isle knitting are established, you will be ready to tackle the project that follows, which is a colorful tablet case.

True Fair-Isle knitting

A lot of knitting that is called "fair isle" is not strictly Fair Isle in the true sense of the term. Traditional Fair-Isle knitting employs lots of very small repeated patterns that only ever use two colors in a row. Knitting that employs more than two colors in a row is really stranded knitting—or

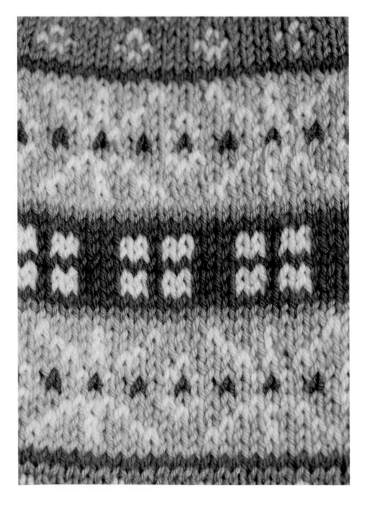

Jacquard, a rather old-fashioned weaving term that you may see used in vintage pattern books.

So what is it about this type of knitting that has given it such widespread appeal and longevity? As in traditional cable knitting (see page 96), the lanolin in natural wool offers a degree of water resistance, but the stranding of the yarns along the back of the work is also one of the keys to its popularity because it adds an extra layer of the wool behind the knitted piece. When these layers are knitted from Shetland or Highland wool it creates an extremely warm fabric: this wool is known for its durability and ability to "felt" or matt together to create a completely cold-resistant, solid fabric.

Fair Isle is a small island off the coast of Scotland, and the traditional patterns of the Shetland Isles also have a long, similar heritage. We are all very familiar with these type of patterns: traditionally they are worked in the natural colors of the hardy sheep that are native to the area or in soft, contemporary heathered tones.

Many other Northern European countries boast a similar historical knitting culture, with remarkably similar designs and techniques. Estonia, for instance, has a tradition of making patterned gloves and socks, while Scandinavia has its own set of traditional motifs that are worked in a similar way.

Keeping strands neat

When working with only two colors, place one ball to your right and one to your left; this helps to avoid excessive tangling.

To maintain an even gauge (tension), spread stitches evenly on the needles so the float will be the right length for the fabric to sit flat. If you work too tightly and pull on the strands, your work will pucker and curl, which can be hard to rectify once established. Strands that are too loose are simpler to correct, but can be time consuming.

Stranding

With intarsia, a separate ball is used for each area of color; in Fair Isle, one ball per color is used per row, and the yarn not in use is carried across the back and picked up as needed. So you will need to manage several strands of yarn running along the wrong side of the work without creating a big tangle. To change color in a row without creating a hole, twist the yarns together before dropping one and changing to the next (see Workshop 16, page 138) and a similar principle applies with Fair Isle. Carrying the yarn across the back creates strands or floats, and the technique is known as stranding; it is best used when color changes are close together so that the strands are not too long.

Stranding on the right side of the work
For the purposes of this tutorial we will assume that the knit side is the right side of the work, and the purl side is the wrong side.

Stranding on the wrong side of the work
The technique is very similar when worked on the wrong side. In circular knitting, however, all rows are worked on the right side.

1 To strand yarns over short areas when working a right-side row, knit up to the first color change, then drop the first color and pick up the second, stranding the yarn over the dropped tail of the first yarn.

2 Knit with the second color, keeping the yarn not in use stranded along the back of the work. Keep the working stitches spread out on the needle so that the float created is the right size. At the next color change pick up the first color, pull it gently but not firmly, and drop the second. Keep the yarns in the same position that they fall, one running above the other, all along the row if you can. This makes for a neater back to the work and also helps maintain an evenness to the knit side.

1 Purl to the point of the first color change, then drop the first color and pick up the second, stranding the second color over the top of the first. Purl with the second color until you are ready for the next color change, spreading the working stitches out on the needle so that the stranded yarn runs at the right gauge (tension). On this side of the work you should find that the yarns sit quite naturally, compared to the right side.

2 At the point of the next color change, drop the second color and pick up the first one again, pulling on it gently but not firmly, then purl the next stitch. Keep the yarns in the same position as they fall, as you did when working on the right side.

Stranding practice

To put this technique into practice, cast on 31 stitches in the first color (yarn A), and work two rows in stockinette (stocking) stitch. Join in the second color (yarn B) where needed and work the seven rows of Chart 1 below, stranding the yarns across the back of the work as directed on page 145.

Work a two-row stockinette (stocking) stitch stripe in a third color, then work the seven rows of Chart 1 once again. If you feel confident at 2-color stranding now, knit four rows of stockinette (stocking) stitch in yarn A, so that you are ready to work the weaving practice that follows.

Chart 1

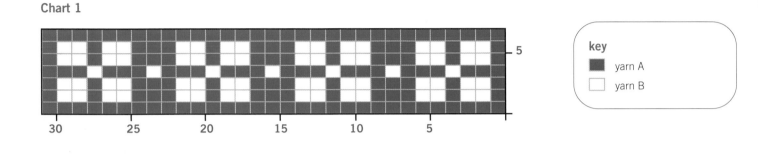

key

▇ yarn A

☐ yarn B

Weaving

If the gap between color changes is more than five stitches—or as few as three stitches on thicker yarns—you need to weave the stranded yarns together at intervals. This technique is not to be confused with weaving in tails—to weave the yarns, they are twisted together on the back during the knitting, which shortens the loose float thread, making it much less likely to become caught.

To twist the yarns when working a right-side row

To twist the yarns when working a wrong-side row

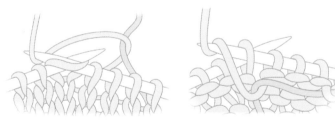

As with intarsia, try to alternate the direction you twist in to avoid developing great tangles on the rear of the work. You can either choose to alternate direction every other twist, or every other row. Weaving in should be applied when there are more than two yarns running at the back of the work. It becomes harder to manage the yarns as you work with more of them, so maintaining the gauge (tension) and alternating the twists is essential to keep your sanity. As with intarsia, Fair-Isle knitting is not a swift process but the results are stunning. Once you become used to this twisting motion you can apply it to weave in yarn tails at the start and end of rows. Weave the tail and out of 4–5 stitches to secure it, thereby eliminating lots of sewing in at the end.

Weaving practice

Returning to the stranding sample you made earlier, join in yarn B and work the five rows of Chart 2. You will need to weave the float yarns over larger gaps between color changes, but strand the yarns over shorter gaps. For more practice, work a second repeat of the five rows before binding (casting) off.

Chart 2

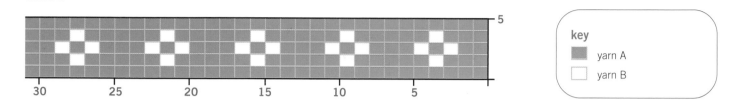

key
■ yarn A
□ yarn B

Mixing Fair Isle and plain or intarsia knitting

Fair-isle knitting has a tendency to be narrower than plain stockinette (stocking) stitch because of the strands running at the back, which also make it a thicker fabric. Many knitting patterns call for a blend of Fair-Isle areas and plain knitting, but there will be a difference in gauge (tension) between these two types of fabric because of the above factor. To compensate for this, work the plain areas on a smaller knitting needle to bring the width of the plain knitting closer to that of the Fair Isle. You may also need to work Fair-Isle and intarsia techniques within the same piece. Intarsia is also wider than Fair Isle, so again—if the areas are very separate such as a Fair-Isle border and an intarsia central motif—use smaller needles for the area not worked in Fair Isle.

Charts and Fair Isle: working with repeats

Charts for Fair-Isle designs usually show a section to be repeated over the piece. In fact, there may be several different small charts, with each to be repeated across the whole row in sequence. Look at the small charts below, which will create the Fair-Isle design shown in the photo opposite. All the rows of Chart A are worked once in repeat across the whole width of the whole piece, then several rows of stockinette (stocking) stitch are worked before all the rows of Chart B are worked, again repeated over the whole width. Then a few more rows of stockinette (stocking) stitch, before all the rows of Chart C are worked, repeated over the whole row. Then after a few more rows of stockinette (stocking) stitch the sequence begins again from chart B.

This is a common method of abbreviating charts; since the three patterns each have a different number of stitches, it would require a huge chart to show how they all fit together. Cutting each design down to a small repeat is also less daunting to follow.

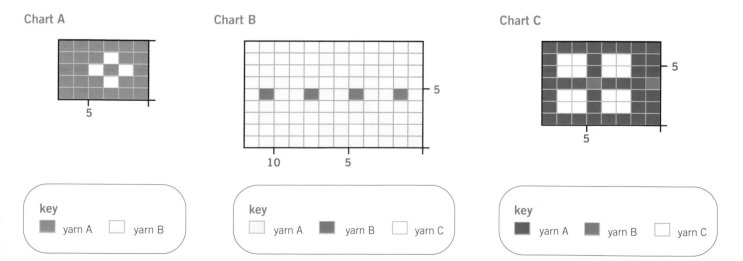

Chart A

key
■ yarn A □ yarn B

Chart B

key
□ yarn A ■ yarn B □ yarn C

Chart C

key
■ yarn A ■ yarn B □ yarn C

Charts and symbols

In modern knitting patterns, colorwork charts are usually shown in color, with an appropriate color in each square to denote the yarn color you should knit that stitch in. With much older vintage patterns, however, you may find a black-and-white chart full of symbols rather than colored squares. If this seems confusing, and chances are it will, then make a photocopy of it and color the squares in using something light such as colored pencils, so that you can still see the individual squared lines.

Following different sizes on a chart

We have already learned that to follow an individual size in a knitting pattern you must select the appropriate number from a set, with larger sizes in parentheses, according to the size you are making; for example, "Cast on 20(**22**:24:**26**:28) sts." When a chart over the full width of a piece is given in a pattern with different size options, there will be a series of darker lines at either side, each one showing where to begin and end the chart for the particular size you are working. This can be another confusing feature if you are not conversant with following charts. Again, just photocopy the chart and either darken the lines for the size you are making and cross out the rest, or use a highlighter pen to color in the very last square of each row for the size you are working. This will give you a clear indication of where to start working the chart and where to stop. It also helps when you to compare your work to the chart to check you have worked it correctly.

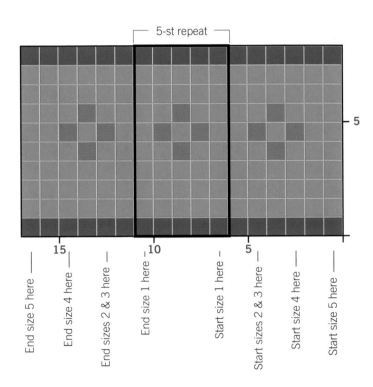

Using the chart

On the chart above you would need to choose the right starting position for the size you are making from the options across the bottom, then work the necessary number of repeats of the center 5-stitch repeat for your size, then continue along to the appropriate end point for that size.

Fair Isle tablet case

This cheerful case will fit a Kindle or other small tablet. It has no shaping but plenty of stranded Fair-Isle patterning so it offers a good opportunity to practice this technique and follow a chart—and is a good way to use up odds and ends of bright-colored yarn.

techniques used

Stranded Fair-Isle knitting

Following a chart

Blocking

Mattress stitch to join

yarn

Cascade 220 Superwash wool, (100% wool) light worsted (DK) yarn

1 x 3½ oz (100 g) ball—220 yd (200 m— each of shades 1973 Seafoam Heather (A), 871 White (C), 811 Como blue (D), 827 Coral (E)

Rowan Baby Merino Silk DK (66% merino wool/34% silk) light worsted (DK) yarn

1 x 1¾ oz (50 g) ball—147 yd (135 m)—of shade 698 Jewel (B)

needles

Pair of US size 6 (4 mm) needles

other materials

Blunt darning needle

One button approx. 1 in. (2.5 cm) diameter

Approx. 16½ x 6½ in. (42 x 16.5 cm) of cotton fabric for lining

Matching thread and sewing needle

finished measurements

Length: 8¼ in. (21 cm)

Width: 6 in. (15.5 cm)

gauge (tension)

22 sts and 25 rows to 4 in. (10 cm) working Fair-Isle patt using US size 6 (4 mm) needles.

abbreviations

beg	beginning
k	knit
p	purl
patt	pattern
RS	right side
st(s)	stitch(es)
WS	wrong side

To make the case

Using yarn A, cast on 36 sts.

Work 6 rows in k1, p1 rib.

Join yarn B and begin chart, joining in yarns where
indicated and remembering to read chart from right to left
on RS rows, and from left to right on WS rows. Work in st st
until end of chart.

Fold line:

Using only yarn A, k 1 row, p 3 rows, and k 1 row.

Now work chart again, but this time from top
downward—beg with Row 44—until you reach the bottom.

Using only yarn A, work 6 rows in k1, p1 rib.

Bind (cast) off in rib.

Fastening loop

Using yarn A, cast on 6 sts. Work 16 rows in k1, p1 rib.
Bind (cast) off.

Finishing

Block piece by steam method (see Workshop 1, page 26).
Weave in all loose tails.

Making up

Fold fastening loop so that edges cross over, like a ribbon
loop. Using yarn A in a darning needle, stitch edges to
central 6 sts of one ribbed edge of main piece. Make sure
the loop hangs down in front, in a central position.

Fold main piece in half horizontally and join side seams with mattress stitch (see page 56), using a length of yarn A. With another length of yarn A, stitch button onto other rib edge to correspond with loop fastening.
Lining:
Iron the lining fabric. Fold in half horizontally, RS together. Turn over top edges and pin a hem allowance of approximately ⅜ in. (1 cm). Sew hems.
Pin side seams with a seam allowance of approximately ⅜ in. (1 cm) and sew. Snip corners, fasten off any loose tails securely. Place lining inside knitted tablet case and pin in place. Using a length of sewing thread, stitch lining discreetly with small stitches along top to attach it.

NOTE: this case is knitted from the top downward, starting with the rows of ribbing that form the opening. The image on page 150, opposite, shows how the finished case looks when it has been turned up the other way.

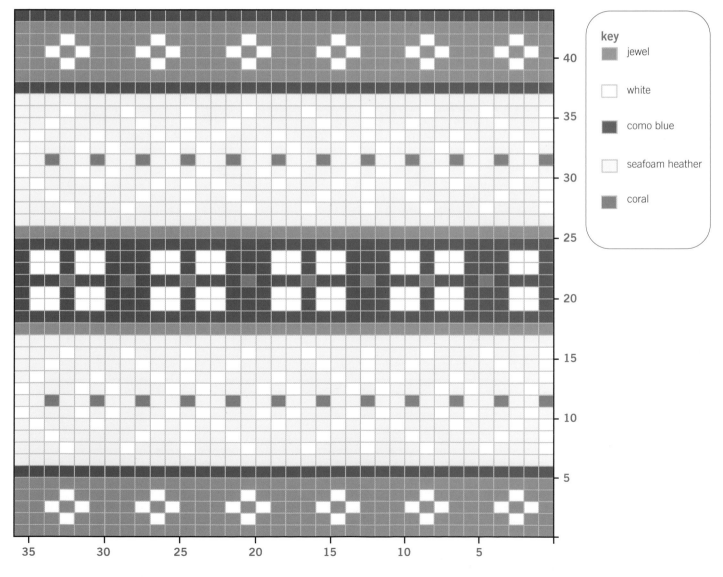

key
- ■ jewel
- □ white
- ■ como blue
- □ seafoam heather
- ■ coral

Workshop 18

Embellishing your knits

It is time to learn some creative ways to decorate your work. In this workshop we look at creating a design with beads knitted into the fabric, simple embroidery stitches that can be worked on knitted fabric, and a clever way of imitating knit stitches. Finally there is a technique to elongate stitches, suitable for adding detail to a host of items. The project to try out some of these techniques is a sophisticated Clutch Purse.

Using beads

This is a skill that some knitters find daunting. You need to plan ahead and prepare the yarn and beads, but the technique itself is simple to learn and produces impressive results. Adding beads to a project will add to its weight; for the beaded purse this is a positive factor, but it may detract from other items. Beaded knitting also tends to be wider than non-beaded knitting, so if you mix the two types of fabric you may need to increase or decrease stitches to regulate the difference in size.

Many beaded designs use charts to indicate where to knit in a bead. You need at least one more stitch in each row than the number of beads to be knitted in because with some techniques the beads sit between two stitches, so to knit in 36 beads you must have at least 37 stitches.

Count out the number of beads you need according to the chart. You need to thread all the beads onto the yarn at the start or you will have to cut the yarn to add more. It is better to use beads with holes only a little larger than the girth of the yarn because if the holes are much larger the knitting will be looser and the beads will move about. If the beads are in a sequence of colors, thread the last one onto the yarn first, so that it will be knitted in last.

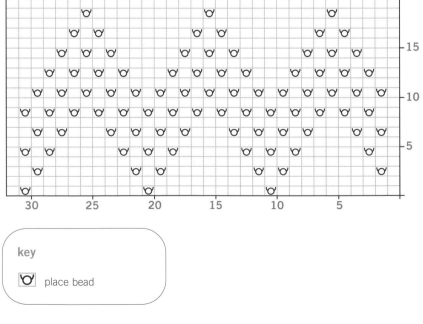

key

⬭ place bead

If your yarn is thin enough to accommodate the holes in your beads, loop the yarn through a small length of sewing cotton and then thread both ends of the cotton into a sewing needle. Push the beads onto the needle and then down onto the yarn in sequence.

If your yarn is too thick for the holes in the beads you are using, then thread the beads onto very fine sewing thread and wind this back up into a spool. Knit the beaded thread together with the main yarn, to give the appearance of the beads being knitted in to the main yarn.

Knitting with beads

Once you have prepared your beaded yarn you are ready to start knitting. It is far, far easier to work with beads on purl stitches, or in a stitch pattern such as seed (moss) or garter stitch, because the horizontal bar of the purl stitch lends itself more easily to the addition of a bead. You can usually purl any stitches that have a bead attached, even if the unbeaded surrounding stitches are all knit stitches, because the bead itself will cover up any visible jarring of the stitches and hide the odd purl stitch.

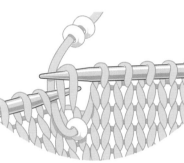

To knit with your beads, work as normal up to the first point where a bead is indicated. Work the next stitch, then bring a bead to the front of the work, and work the next stitch to secure it in position, ensuring that the bead sits on the front of the work.

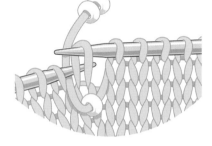

It is possible to work beads into knit stitches but it is a lot harder to make sure they lie straight and even because the V structure of a knit stitch means the bead has to lie on one leg of the V. An alternative option is to slip the stitch behind the bead, as shown above.

Simple beaded sample

To practice working with beads, thread at least 60 beads onto a ball of yarn, using one of the methods outlined above.

Cast on 30 sts and work 3 rows in stockinette (stocking) stitch, ending on a knit row.
Next row: P1, [place bead at front of work, p2] to end.
Next row: Knit all sts to end.
Next row: [P2, place bead at front of work] to last st, p1.
Next row: Knit all sts to end.
Rep these 4 rows once again, then stop to see your work. You should have created a spaced overall bead design, with all the beads sitting at the front of the work.

This technique will be used in the Beaded Clutch Purse on page 156, but in a slightly different arrangement of beads, to create a zigzag pattern.

Swiss darning

Also known as duplicate stitch, this is a useful technique to learn. Not only is it a very effective way to embellish your work, it can also be used to cover up small mistakes in colorwork patterns or to repair threadbare or damaged knitting. Swiss darning is more effective when worked on the knit side of stockinette (stocking) stitch, but it can be worked on purl stitches once you have learned the method. Essentially the technique is very simple, because you are following the path of the knitted stitch beneath.

To practice this technique, work up a small piece of plain stockinette (stocking) stitch and then Swiss darn a horizontal line in another color, or try working a small motif such as a simple cross or diamond.

1 Thread up a blunt darning needle with a length of contrast yarn. With the RS of the knitted piece facing you, insert the needle into the back of the work and bring it out at the front, at the base of the V of the stitch to embroider over. Pass the needle behind both bars of the V of the stitch above the one you are working on, and pull the yarn through.

2 Insert the needle back into the space where you began the stitch, at the base of the knitted V you have covered.

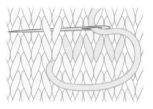

3 Try to work from right to left, as shown here, because the sewing will be imitating the natural path of the knitted row beneath. Finish off your loose yarn tails by weaving them in as normal.

Using Swiss darning

if you have accidentally knitted a stitch in the wrong color, rather than unravel the knitting you can thread up a length of the correct yarn and Swiss darn over the mistake. This only works for individual stitches or very few stitches; it will start to show over too many adjacent stitches, because the embroidered stitches are slightly raised from the background. Swiss darning is also useful for adding a single vertical line of stitches, or an occasional touch of contrast color—it is less time-consuming and simpler than using a second color for small areas.

Other embroidery stitches

There is a range of other hand-stitch techniques that can be used to embellish knitted fabrics after they are finished. Here are some ideas that you might want to try out:

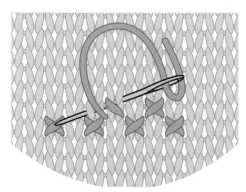

Cross stitch
This works very well because the diagonals of the cross blend well with the structure of knit stitches. Cross stitch works best on the knit side of stockinette (stocking) stitch, but it can also be worked reasonably successfully over a row of garter stitch or seed (moss) stitch.

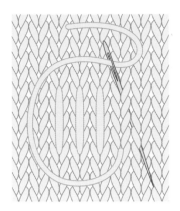

Running stitch and straight stitch

Running stitch simply involves threading the needle in and out of the base fabric to create a line of stitches. Straight stitch is very similar—single stitches are worked vertically or radiating outward. Try using thicker yarn than the base knitting, or a Lurex yarn that will glint in and out of the main fabric. Running stitch works well on most knitted fabric and can also be employed to gather up finer knitting to create a smocking effect or ruching.

Chain stitch

This is great way to add linear details or outlines using a very familiar stitch. Bring the needle up through the fabric, then insert it in the same place and bring it up again a bit further along. Loop the end of the yarn around the needle tip before pulling through. It can also be worked as individual stitches in a circle to create a simple flower shape.

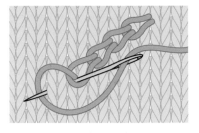

Stem stitch

This consists of small, slanting stitches worked close together and overlapping slightly to create a continuous line. It is a good way to create raised outlines or add leaf or petal shapes onto a plain knit ground.

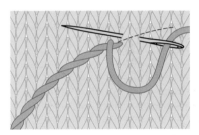

One last trick: elongating stitches

This technique is not embroidery, but is too much fun not to include. Work stockinette (stocking) stitch with 30 stitches and 8 rows, ending with a purl row.

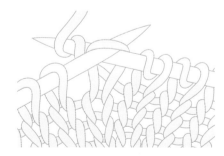

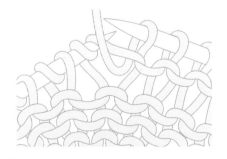

1 Wrap the yarn as if to knit the next stitch, but instead of wrapping just once, wrap it over an extra time before working the stitch. Complete the knit stitch as normal, then repeat the double wrapping for each remaining stitch. It will now look as if you have 60 stitches on your right needle. Turn.

2 Insert the right needle into the first loop on the left needle, as if to purl. Purl the stitch off, allowing the second loop to fall off the left needle as you push off the first one. Repeat for all other stitches. You should now have 30 stitches again. Pull down gently on the bottom of the sample to stretch out the row.

The stitches in the row just worked will look longer than those in the rows below and may be a little looser. This effect can be exploited by working the double-wrapped rows in a contrast color, or by working every row as a double-wrapped row to create a mesh-like knitted fabric. Garter stitch also works well with this technique.

You can wrap the yarn more than twice if you wish: the more times you wrap, the longer the resultant stitches—although the fabric will be correspondingly looser and less stable, and stitches will be prone to catching and distorting. Up to four wraps per stitch is generally practical, so try wrapping a row of stitches three or four times, using the sample you have made.

Beaded clutch purse

This small, elegant purse uses luxurious yarn but only needs one ball, so it is not an expensive project. Choose toning beads—glass beads add a pleasing weight. Finally, choose a silky lining to suit the vintage look.

techniques used

Threading beads onto the yarn

Following a beading chart

Mattress stitch to join

yarn

Rowan Truesilk DK (100% silk) light worsted (DK) yarn

1 x 1¾ oz (50 g) ball—164 yd (150 m)—of shade 333 Hush

needles

Pair of US size 5 (3.75 mm) needles

other materials

342 beads, 6mm glass

Blunt darning needle

10¼ x 11 in. (26 x 28 cm) of lining fabric

Sewing needle and thread

4 medium-size black snap fasteners

finished measurements

9½ x 5½ in. (24.5 x 14 cm)

gauge (tension)

24 sts and 44 rows to 4 in. (10 cm) working chevron patt using US size 5 (3.75 mm) needles.

abbreviations

beg	beginning
k	knit
p	purl
patt	pattern
rep	repeat
RS	right side
st(s)	stitch(es)
st st	stockinette (stocking) stitch
WS	wrong side

Special stitch note: beadwork

Purl beaded stitches and knit stitches between, so that the beads sit on the horizontal bars of the purl stitches.

To place a bead, bring yarn forward between needles to RS of work, slide bead up to needle, p stitch, take yarn back between needles to WS.

To make the purse
Thread beads onto yarn (see page 153).
Cast on 59 sts.

Rows 1–2: K to end.
Rows 3–7: Work in st st, beg with a k row.
Rows 8–10: K to end.

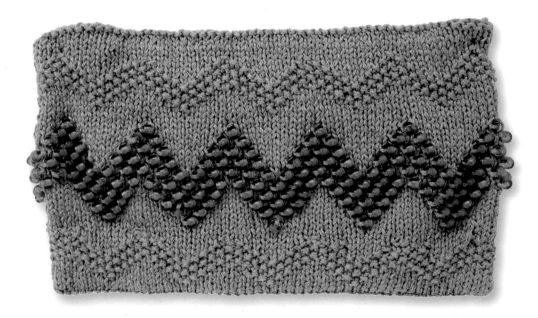

Chart 1

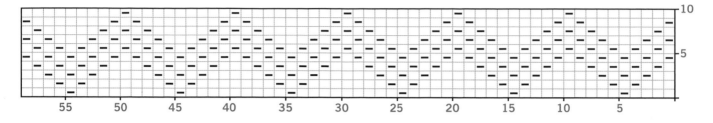

Chart 2

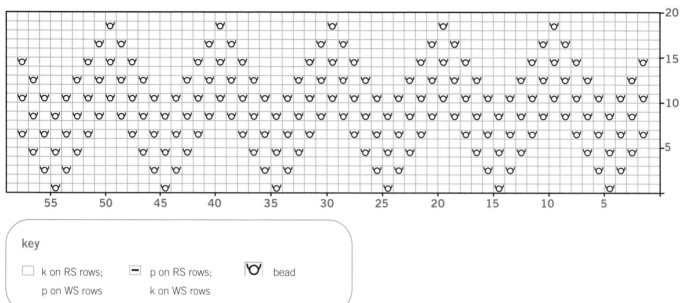

key

☐ k on RS rows;
p on WS rows

▬ p on RS rows;
k on WS rows

🝓 bead

Rows 11–15: Work in st st, beg with a k row.

Rows 16–25: Work 10 rows of Chart 1, beg with a WS row.

Rows 26–28: Work in st st, beg with a p row.

Rows 29–48: Work 20 rows of Chart 2, beg with a RS row.

Rows 49–50: Work in st st, beg with a k row.

Rows 51–60: Work 10 rows of Chart 1, beg with a RS row.

Rows 61–65: Work in st st, beg with a k row.

Row 66: K to end (bottom fold formed).

Rows 67–71: Work in st st, beg with a k row.

Rows 72–81: Work 10 rows of Chart 1 in reverse from Row 10 to Row 1, beg with a WS row.

Rows 82–83: Work in st st, beg with a p row.

Rows 84–103: Work 20 rows of Chart 2 in reverse from Row 20 to Row 1, beg with a WS row..

Rows 104–106: Work in st st, beg with a p row.

Rows 107–116: Work 10 rows of Chart 1 in reverse from Row 10 to Row 1, beg with a WS row.

Rows 117–121: Work in st st, beg with a k row.

Rows 122–124: K to end.

Rows 125–129: Work in st st, beg with a k row.

Rows 130–131: K to end.

Bind (cast) off.

Finishing

Weave in tails. Fold piece in half horizontally and mattress stitch the side seams together very neatly.

Lining:

Fold top edges over by ⅜ in. (1 cm) twice to make a double hem and sew in place. Fold the lining in half horizontally along center, right sides together, and sew side seams with a ⅜ in. (1 cm) seam allowance. Push lining inside purse. Fold garter st edging over edges of lining, then sew down with very small stitches along edge of each lip through all fabrics.

Stitch a snap fastener at each end toward the side seam, and the other evenly in between.

Workshop 19

Buttons, buttonholes, and other fastenings

This short workshop is rather a skills top-up of techniques covered earlier in the book, coupled with a look at how to apply these to create buttonhole fastenings. The project to put some of these techniques into practice is a cute pair of baby shoes.

Buttons and buttonholes

In Workshop 9 (see page 80) we learned how to bind (cast) off and cast on again in the middle of a row to create an opening, and this technique can be employed to create buttonholes. Buttonholes are usually worked horizontally, even when the button band is worked vertically.

Before working a set of buttonholes you need to choose the buttons. A good knitting pattern will give the diameter of the recommended button size, but some patterns are less specific. If you are devising your own pattern it's best to choose your button and then make a series of test buttonholes in a sample piece worked in the same orientation as the button band. The button should fit snugly but not too easily through the buttonhole, but bear in mind that knitting has a natural stretch and buttonholes used time and again will tend to expand slightly. So it is worth making a buttonhole that is initially somewhat tight, because it will eventually open up a little.

For the smallest buttonholes, working two stitches together with a yarn over afterward to retain the stitch count is sufficient. This will accommodate a small button or a bead used as a button. Larger horizontal buttonholes can be worked by binding (casting) off a few stitches and then casting them back on using a firm cast on method on the following row.

Working a standard horizontal buttonhole
Cast on 10 sts, then work10 rows in k1, p1 ribbing.
Buttonhole row: [K1, p1] twice, bind (cast) off 2 sts, [k1, p1] twice.
Next row: [K1, p1] twice, swap over the needles to place the needle containing the stitches you have just worked in your left hand. Cast on 2 sts using the cable cast-on method, but before you place the last cast-on st back on the left needle, bring the yarn to the front. Switch the needles back to normal; [k1, p1] twice.
Work a further 10 rows in k1, p1 ribbing, then work another buttonhole as above.

If you examine the buttonholes you have produced you will see that they are a bit flimsy; to reinforce them you can add a ring of buttonhole stitch (see page 160). Button bands are often knitted on a smaller size needle to retain tightness and neatness.

Placing buttons

It is possible to create vertical buttonholes, but they are slightly harder to work. You must work each side of the buttonhole separately, holding the stitches not in use, before joining the two groups together at the top, at the end of the buttonhole. This is a far less common method to use, and would be prone to stretching outward.

Buttonholes and buttons do not have to be spaced out evenly. More creative options would be grouping them in pairs, with a larger space between each pair, or placing more buttons toward the top and fewer below, as on a smock. Consider the end use of the garment, then decide on how to arrange the fastenings.

Reinforcing buttonholes with stitching

Adding an extra layer of firm stitching will increase the strength of a buttonhole; a simple blanket or buttonhole stitch works well, if stitches are very close together, as in the diagram.

Button loops

Another fastening mechanism that is remarkably simple to work is a loop construction worked at the very edge of a button band. Crochet is the simplest way to accomplish this: by crocheting a tight chain loop at intervals, you can make a very quick and easy fastening. You can also create a length of French knitting (also called I-cord) and stitch it along the edge of the button band, forming loops at intervals.

Choosing buttons

When choosing buttons consider the size, color, and material in relation to your yarn. Buttons are often matched to a yarn color, so for accurate matching take a small amount of yarn when you go to buy them. On a Fair-Isle or intarsia design you might pick out one of the contrast colors in the pattern. On paler colors, white or clear buttons will always work well, and natural tones will be enhanced by cream, beige, or pewter shades.

Consider the yarn you have used, and the purpose of the item. If you have used a luxurious silky yarn it would be a shame to use cheap buttons, but childrenswear benefits from the practicality and safety of plastic buttons or wooden toggles. There are many beautiful handcrafted buttons available, so have fun seeking out something worthy of all your hard work. Another option is to use large beads instead of conventional buttons. Think creatively—many everyday things can be used as buttons, as long as you can attach them to the knitting.

Making your own buttons

If you want buttons in the same yarn as the knitting, the easiest option is to crochet small bead shapes, or round discs worked in a very tight gauge. You can also knit small squares of fabric and use them on self-covering buttons, which are available in kits.

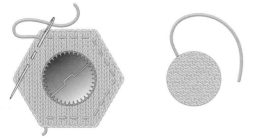

In the project that follows, a pair of Baby Cross-strap Shoes, there are only two buttonholes and buttons per shoe to deal with, but the project in Workshop 20 will really give you chance to practice your skills in an accomplished piece.

Sewing on buttons

To attach buttons to knitting, use a needle thin enough to pass through the hole in the button when threaded up with the yarn. The yarn can be the same color as the button band, or a deliberate contrast. Stitch through the holes several times in an oversewing motion and make sure the tails are very securely fastened afterward. Buttons on knitwear are prone to working loose, so keep a little yarn for later repairs.

When you are ready to sew on buttons, place the two bands side by side and mark the empty button band with a safety pin or a small stitch to match the buttonhole, so that you know where to stitch the buttons.

Baby cross-strap shoes

These soft baby shoes are quick to work up and are great for little feet that are between booties and rigid shoes. They are decorated with Swiss darning and chain stitch, and have eyelet buttonholes on the straps.

techniques used

Swiss darning

Chain stitch

Simple buttonholes

Paired decreases

Oversewing and mattress stitch to join

yarn

Rowan wool cotton 4-ply, (50% cotton, 50% merino wool) fingering (4-ply) yarn

1 x 1¾ oz (50 g) ball—197 yd (180 m)—each of shades 489 Satsuma (A), 483 White (B), 493 Rich (C)

needles

Pair of US size 2 (2.75 mm) needles

other materials

Blunt darning needle

Four small buttons, ⅜ in. (1 cm) diameter

Size

To fit baby 3–6 (6–9:9–12) months

gauge (tension)

26 sts and 60 rows to 4 in. (10 cm) working garter stitch using US size 2 (2.75 mm) needles.

abbreviations

beg	beginning
dec	decrease
g st	garter stitch
inc	increase
k	knit
k2tog	knit 2 stitches together
psso	pass slipped stitch over
rem	remaining
rep	repeat
RS	right side
sl	slip
st(s)	stitch(es)
st st	stockinette (stocking) stitch
WS	wrong side
yo	yarn over

To make the shoes

Right sole:

Using yarn C, cast on 12(14:16) sts.

Work 2 rows in g st.

Next row (inc row): K1, inc 1, k to last 2 sts, inc 1 in next st, k last st. 14(16:18) sts

Work 4 rows in g st.

Next row (inc row): K1, inc 1, k to last 2 sts, inc 1 in next st, k last st. 16(18:20) sts

Work 8(12:16) rows in g st without shaping.

Next row: K1, k2tog, k to last 3 sts, k2tog, k1**. Work 6 rows in g st without shaping.

Next row: K to last 4 sts, k2tog, k2. 13(15:17) sts

Work 5(7:9) rows in g st without shaping.

Next row: K to last 4 sts, k2tog, k2. 12(14:16) sts

***Work 6(10:14) rows in g st without shaping.

Next row: K1, k2tog, k to last 3 sts, k2tog, k1.

Work 6(10:14) rows in g st without shaping.

Next row: K1, k2tog, k to last 3 sts, k2tog, k1.

Work 1 row in g st without shaping.

Next row: K1, k2tog, k to last 3 sts, k2tog, k1.

Bind (cast) off 3(4:5) sts at beg of each of next 2 rows.

Left sole:

Work as for Right Sole to **.

Next row: K2, k2tog, k to end.

Work 5(7:9) rows in g st without shaping.

Next row: K2, k2tog, k to end.

Now work as for right sole from *** to end.

Cross straps

(make 2 alike)

Using yarn A, cast on 66(72:80) sts.

Work 3 rows in g st without shaping.

Next row: K2, yo, k2tog, k to last 4 sts, sl 1, k1, psso, yo, k2.

Work 4 more rows in g st without shaping.

Bind (cast) off.

Shoe front

(make 2 alike)

Using yarn A, cast on 84(**96**:108) sts.

Work 1(1:2) row(s) in g st.

Change to yarn B. Work 2 rows in g st.

Change back to yarn A. Work 2(**2**:4) rows in g st.

Next row (dec row): K31(**36**:41), k2tog, k1, sl 1, k1, psso, k12(**14**:16), k2tog, k1, sl 1, k1, psso, k31(**36**:41).

Work 3 rows in g st without shaping.

Next row (dec row): K31(**36**:41), k2tog, k1, sl 1, k1, psso, k8(**10**:12), k2tog, k1, sl 1, k1, psso, k31(**36**:41).

Work 3 rows in g st without shaping.

Shape tongue:

Bind (cast) off first 31(**36**:41) sts, k next 13(**15**:17) sts, turn.

Work 7 rows in st st over center 14(**16**:18) sts only, then 2 rows in g st.

Bind (cast) off these 14(**16**:18) sts.

Rejoin yarn and bind (cast) off rem 31(**36**:41) sts.

Finishing

Weave in all loose tails.

Embroidery trims:

Thread a length of yarn B into the darning needle. Following the photograph as an guide, chain stitch a heart motif on each sole.

Thread up a length of yarn C. Again using the photograph as a guide, Swiss darn a heart motif on the tongue section of each shoe front.

Weave in all remaining loose tails.

Making up

Pin one shoe front to one sole, with RS facing. Starting at narrower end of sole (back of shoe), pin along edge, making sure that tongue section sits lined up with wider front section of sole. Continue back to narrow part of sole. Thread up a length of yarn A and stitch the pieces together using small, neat oversewing stitches (see page 27). Finally, mattress stitch (see page 55) the two ends together at back of shoe. Rep with other sole and shoe front.

To shape shoe front, place tongue so three stitches of the st st section sit under adjacent g sts at either side, creating a gentle slope and forming a triangular shape. A small flap of st st will be inside shoe—see photograph as a guide to stitch it down, using oversewing on WS of shoe.

To attach cross straps, fold one strap piece in half to find the center. Pin this to back of one shoe and continue pinning around side of shoe to front (pinning at the edge). Rep for other side of shoe front, then thread up a length of yarn A and neatly mattress stitch the strap to the shoe front along the pinned seam. Rep for the other shoe.

Thread up a length of yarn A and position the buttons as shown in the photograph, so that straps can cross over and buttonholes match up. Stitch each button down. Weave in all remaining loose tails.

Workshop 20

Finishing touches and a few additional skills

We have now covered all the major topics and techniques to enable you to knit proficiently and confidently. In this final workshop, we look at a few extra skills: how to cast on using three new methods and how to make patch and inset pockets. The final project, a child's cardigan, pulls together many of the skills from throughout this book.

Some new ways to cast on

Throughout this book we have used the cable cast-on method, which is a useful all-rounder. However, there are several alternative ways to cast on that suit particular purposes best. Here are two more to add to your skill base.

Revising how to pick up stitches

We have not needed to pick up stitches for some time in our projects in this book, so as the following cardigan project requires you to pick up and knit the button bands it may be time for a quick recap. See Workshop 10, Picking up stitches, pages 89–91.

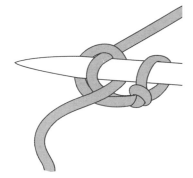

Thumb cast on

Many knitters think this is the easiest way to cast on. It involves knitting into a loop made around the thumb to make a stitch on the needle. Leave a long tail of about ¾ in. (2 cm) per stitch to be cast on and then make a slip knot; the slip knot will be the first stitch.

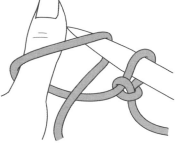

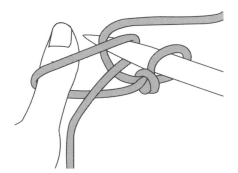

1 Holding the needle and the yarn from the ball in your right hand, use the free tail of yarn to make a loop around your left thumb while at the same time keeping the yarn taut between the third and fourth fingers of your left hand. Insert the needle tip into the loop.

2 Bring the yarn from the ball up between your thumb and the needle then take it around the needle, as shown above.

3 Draw the yarn through to make a stitch on the needle, then release the loop from the left thumb and gently pull on the yarn tail to tighten the stitch on the needle.

Slit or inset pockets

This type of pocket is slightly more complicated to work but there are no skills involved that you have not already learned, and with the help of stitch holders and a little patience it is worth the extra effort. It offers a professional, neat finish that is more suitable for tailored garments. Its disadvantages include that you need to plan ahead on where to position it and also decide on the size in advance: you knit the pocket inner as part of the main garment piece, so once it is made it cannot be changed without unraveling the entire piece.

Making an inset pocket sample

To try out this technique, cast on 30 sts and knit approximately 10 rows in stockinette (stocking) stitch, ending with a purl row.

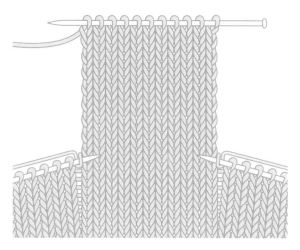

1 Transfer the first 10 sts onto a stitch holder, then join in a new ball of yarn. Knit 10 sts then turn, slipping the last 10 sts onto another stitch holder. Now work 16 rows over the central 10 sts only, ending with a knit row. Fold the central strip of 17 rows over to form a pocket on the back of the work.

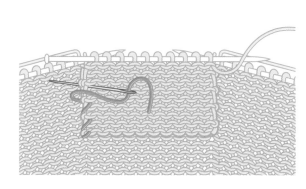

2 Place stitches on the left-hand stitch holder back onto the left needle and knit to end. Turn. Work back across these last stitches and over the top of the pocket stitches, then place the stitches on the right-hand holder back on the left needle and knit these. Sew pocket sides to the rear of the main piece using oversewing (see page 27).

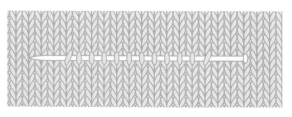

3 If you wish to edge the top of the pocket, then pick up stitches along the top fold of the pocket and knit across them, increasing by one stitch each end for neatness when you come to stitch the sides down. Work this border in a flat pattern such as garter, ribbing, or seed (moss) stitch.

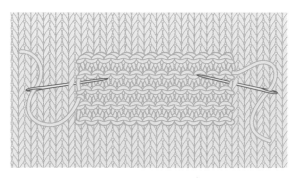

4 Bind (cast) off and then stitch the sides of the border down to the front of the knitting.

College cardigan

This fun and stylish cardigan is suitable for slightly older children. It has an inset pocket with intarsia detailing, raglan shaping, front band, and a shawl collar—perfect for showing off your new knitting skills to full effect!

techniques used

Inset pockets

Intarsia

Adding color using stripes

Following different sizes in a pattern

Ribbing

Shaping

Mattress stitch to join

yarn

Debbie Bliss Cashmerino Aran (55% extra-fine merino wool/33% microfiber/12% cashmere) worsted (Aran) yarn

5(6:7) x 1¾ oz (50 g) balls – 98 yd (90 m) per ball – of shade 205 Denim (A)

4(5:6) x 1¾ oz (50 g) balls – 98 yd (90 m) per ball – of shade 101 Ecru (B)

1 x 1¾ oz (50 g) ball – 98 yd (90 m) – of shade 54 Crimson (C)

needles

One pair of US size 8 (5 mm) needles

other materials

3 x stitch holders

Blunt darning needle

6 buttons to match yarn A, ⅞ in. (2 cm) diameter

size

To fit age

years	7–8	9–10	11–12

Actual measurements

chest

in.	33	35	36½
cm	84	89	93

length to back neck

in.	18	19½	21
cm	46	49.5	53

sleeve length

in.	12½	12½	13¼
cm	32	32	34

gauge (tension)

18 sts and 24 rows to 4 in. (10 cm) working st st using US size 8 (5 mm) needles.

abbreviations

alt	alternate
beg	beginning
cont	continuing
foll	follow(s)ing
k	knit
p	purl
patt	pattern
rem	remaining
RH	right-hand
RS	right side
rep	repeat
sl	slip
ssk	slip, slip, knit 2 stitches together through back loops
st(s)	stitch(es)
st st	stockinette (stocking) stitch
tbl	through back loop
tog	together
WS	wrong side
[]	repeat sequence within square brackets the number of times indicated

To make the cardigan
Back
Using yarn A, cast on 76(**80**:84) sts.
Rib patt.
Row 1: [K2, p1] to last 1(**2**:0) sts, k1(**2**:0).
Row 2: P1(**2**:0), [k1, p2] to end.
Rep these 2 rows in foll color sequence:
2 rows in yarn B.
2 rows in yarn A.
2 rows in yarn C.
2 rows in yarn A.
2 rows in yarn B.
2 rows in yarn A.
Beg with a k row, cont in st st using yarn A. Work straight until Back measures 10¼(**11**:11¾) in./26(**28**:30) cm, ending with a p row.
Begin raglan shaping:
Bind (cast) off 3 sts at beg of next 2 rows. 70(**74**:78) sts
Next row: K2, ssk, k to last 4 sts, k2tog, k2.
Next row: P to end.
Rep these 2 rows until 24(**24**:26) sts rem, ending with a p row.
3rd size only:
Work 2 rows without shaping.
All sizes:
Leave rem sts on st holder.

Right front
Using yarn A, cast on 36(**38**:40) sts.
Rib patt:
Row 1: [K2, p1] to last 0(**2**:1) sts, k0(**2**:1).

Row 2: P0(**2**:1), [k1, p2] to end.
Rep these 2 rows over same sequence as for Back.
Beg with a k row, cont in st st using yarn A, work 4 rows.
Pocket:
Row 1: K9(**10**:11) then work 19 sts of Chart Row 1, k last 8(**9**:10) sts.
This sets position of chart, work rem rows of chart over 19 sts as set.
Fasten off.
Next row (internal pocket): Slip first 9(**10**:11) sts onto a st holder, k19, turn. Work on these 19 sts only.
Work 55 rows in st st in yarn A, ending with a p row.
Fold pocket in half to sit behind main knitting, cut yarn and slip last row of pocket sts onto a st holder.
Rejoin yarn at start of sts on first st holder, k9(**10**:11) sts off st holder, then k 19 pocket sts off second st holder, k last 8(**9**:10) sts.
Work straight until Left Front measures 10¼(**11**:11¾) in./ 26(**28**:30) cm, ending with a k row.
Raglan shaping:
Bind (cast) off 3 sts at beg of next row. 33(**35**:37) sts
Next row: K to last 4 sts, k2tog, k2.
Next row: P to end.
Rep these 2 rows until 25 sts rem, ending with a p row.
Neck shaping:
Next row: K2, ssk, k to last 4 sts, k2tog, k2.
Next row: P to last 4 sts, p2tog tbl, p2
Rep last 2 rows until 16 sts rem, ending with a p row.
Next row: K2, ssk, k to last 4 sts, k2tog, k2.
Next row: P to end.
Rep last 2 rows until 6 sts rem.

Next row: K1, k3tog, k2. 4 sts
Next row: P4.
Next row: K1, k3tog. 2 sts
Next row: P2.
K2tog and fasten off.

Left front

Cast on and work rib patt as for Right Front.
Beg with a k row, work straight in yarn A and st st until Left Front measures 10¼(**11**:11¾) in./26(**28**:30) cm, ending with a p row.
Raglan shaping:
Bind (cast) off 3 sts at beg of next row. 33(**35**:37) sts
Next row: P.
Next row: K2, ssk, k to end.
Rep last 2 rows until 25 sts rem, ending with a p row.
Neck shaping:
Next row: K2, ssk, k to last 4 sts, k2tog, k2.
Next row: P2 p2tog, p to end.
Rep last 2 rows until 16 sts rem, ending with a p row.
Next row: K2, ssk, k to last 4 sts, k2tog, k2.
Next row: P to end.
Rep last 2 rows until 6 sts rem, ending with a p row.
Next row: K2, sl 1, k2tog, psso, k1. 4 sts
Next row: P4.
Next row: K1, sl 1, k2tog, psso. 2 sts
Next row: P2.
K2tog and fasten off.

Right sleeve

Using yarn A, cast on 34(**36**:38) sts.
Row 1: [K2, p1] to last 1(**0**:2) sts, k1(**0**:2).
Row 2: P1(**0**:2), [k1, p2] to end.
Rep these 2 rows over stripe sequence as Back, until all 14 rows are complete.
Change to yarn B.*
Work in st st, and shape as foll:
Inc 1 st at each end of 3rd row and every foll alt row until there are 42(**46**:48) sts, then on every 4th row until there are 68(**72**:76) sts.
Work 3 rows without shaping.
Shape raglan:
Next row: K2, ssk, k to last 4 sts, k2tog, k2.
Next row: P to end.**
Rep last 2 rows until 30 sts rem, ending wit a p row.
Next row: *Bind (cast) off 5 sts, k to last 4 sts, k2tog, k2.
Next row: P to end.
Rep last 2 rows 3 more times.
Bind (cast) off rem 6 sts.

Left sleeve

Work as Right Sleeve to *.
Cont in st st and shape as Right Sleeve but work the foll stripes:
12 rows in yarn B.

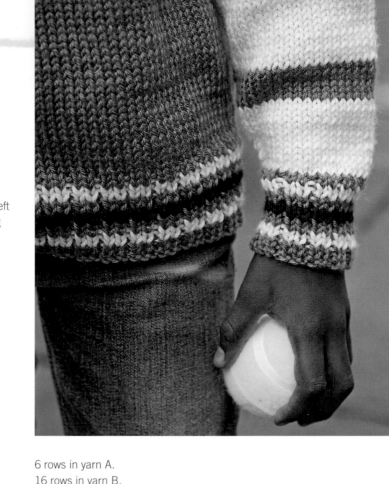

6 rows in yarn A.
16 rows in yarn B.
6 rows in yarn C, then cont in A only to **.
Rep last 2 rows until 30 sts rem, ending with a k row.
Next row: *Bind (cast) off 5 sts, p to end.
Next row: K2, ssk, k to end.
Rep these 2 rows 3 more times.
Next row: P6.
Cast (bind) off.

Button band

With RS facing, using yarn A, pick up and k 60(**64**:68) sts along front edge.
Row 1: [P2, k1] to last 0(**1**:2) sts, p0(**1**:2).
Row 2: K0(**1**:2), [p1, k2] to end.
Rep these 2 rows twice more, then work Row 1 again.
Bind (cast) off loosely in rib (see page 38).

Buttonhole band

Picking up sts on other front edge, work as button band until 3 rib rows have been worked.
Buttonhole row: Patt 2(**4**:6) sts, *bind (cast) off next 2 sts, rib until there are 9 sts on RH needle after bound (cast) off group; rep from * 4 more times, bind (cast) off next 2 sts, rib 1(**3**:5) sts.
Next row: Rib 1(**3**:5) sts, *cast on 2 sts, rib 9; rep from * 4 more times, cast on 2 sts, rib 2(**4**:6) sts.
Work 2 more rows in rib patt.
Bind (cast) off loosely in patt.

Collar

With RS facing and using mattress stitch (see page 55), join raglan seams, sewing last 3 rows below sleeve raglan to bound (cast) off sts on Back and Fronts.

Using yarn A, with RS facing and starting at bound (cast) off edge of front band, pick up and k 16(**16**:17) sts along front neck, 25 sts from right sleeve top, 24(**24**:26) sts from st holder at top of back, 25 sts from top of left sleeve, and 16(**16**:17) sts along left front neck, ending at bound (cast) off edge of front band. 106(**106**:110) sts

Next row: P2, [k1, p2] to end.

Next row: Ssk, [p1, k1] to last 3 sts, p1, k2tog.

Keeping rib correct, dec 1 st at each end of every row until 77(**73**:70) sts rem.

Bind (cast) off loosely in rib.

Finishing

Block all pieces (see page 26).

Thread up a length of yarn A and sew sides of pocket together.

Pin and sew side and sleeve seams using backstitch (see page 33). Sew on buttons.

Weave in all loose tails.

TIP

Choose which side to place buttons, depending on whether the cardigan is for a boy or a girl; boys' clothes usually fasten left over right, girls' clothes right over left.

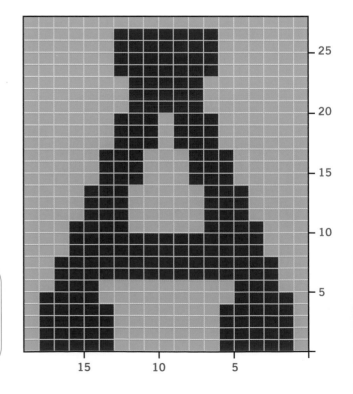

key

■ crimson

■ denim

Suppliers and Resources

US

Yarns:

Cascade
(Cascade)
Online sales
www.cascadeyarns.com

DROPS design
(Drops)
Online sales
www.garnstudio.com

Lion Brand Yarns
(Lion Brand)
Online sales
Tel: +1 800 258 YARN (9276)
www.lionbrand.com

UK

Yarns:

Deramores
(Cascade, Debbie Bliss, Drops, Lion Brand, Sirdar, Rowan)
Online sales
www.deramores.com

Designer Yarns
(Debbie Bliss)
Store locator on website
Tel: +44 (0)1535 664222
www.designeryarns.uk.com

John Lewis
(Debbie Bliss, Patons, Rowan, Sirdar)
Retail stores and online
Tel: +44 (0)3456 049049
Telephone numbers of local stores on website
www.johnlewis.com

loveknitting
(Cascade, Debbie Bliss, Drops Yarns, Lion Brand, Sirdar, Rowan)
www.loveknitting.com

Knitting Fever Inc.
(Debbie Bliss, Sirdar)
Store locator on website
Tel: +1 516 546 3600
www.knittingfever.com

Sirdar c/o HTC
(Sirdar)
307 Simpson Street,
Conover,
North Carolina
NC28613
e-mail: sirdarusa@sirdar.co.uk

WEBS
(Cascade, Debbie Bliss, Rowan)
Online sales
www.yarn.com

Rowan Yarns
(Rowan)
Store locator on website
Tel: +44 (0)1484 681881
www.knitrowan.com

Sirdar Spinning Ltd
(Sirdar)
Store locator on website
Tel: +44 (0) 1924 231682
www.sirdar.co.uk

Wool Warehouse
(Cascade, Debbie Bliss, Drops Yarns, Lion Brand, Sirdar, Rowan)
www.woolwarehouse.co.uk

Accessories/haberdashery:

Hobbycraft
Store locator on website
www.hobbycraft.co.uk

Fred Aldous Ltd
The City
37 Lever St
Manchester M1 1LW
www.fredaldous.co.uk

Westminster Fibers
(Rowan)
Store locator on website
Tel: +1 800 445 9276
www.westminsterfibers.com

Accessories/haberdashery:

Hobby Lobby
www.hobbylobby.com

Jo-Ann
www.joann.com

Michael's
www.michaels.com

Canada

Yarns:

Diamond Yarn
(Debbie Bliss, Sirdar)
Store locator on website
Tel: +1 416 736 6111
www.diamondyarn.com

Westminster Fibers
(Rowan)
Store locator on website
Tel: +1 800 263 2354
www.westminsterfibers.com

Australia

Black Sheep Wool 'n' Wares
(Debbie Bliss, Patons, Sirdar)
Online store
www.blacksheepwool.com.au

Prestige Yarns Pty Ltd
(Debbie Bliss)
Online store
Tel: +61 (0)2 4285 6669
www.prestigeyarns.com.au

Rowan
(Rowan)
Store locator on website
www.knitrowan.com

Sun Spun
(Debbie Bliss, Rowan, Sirdar)
185 Canterbury Road
Canterbury
Victoria
VIC 3126
Tel: +61 (0)3 9830 1609
www.sunspun.com.au

Bibliography and useful websites

You might find the following useful to extend your range of stitch.

201 Knitting Motifs, Blocks, Projects & Ideas (CICO Books, 2010)
A directory of knitting blocks featuring traditional patterns, original motifs, the alphabet and numbers, and new twists on classic stitches.

There are numerous other stitch directories on the market, so check online or in your local bookstore for other options.

Proportional graph paper
As mentioned on page 137, using proportional special knitter's graph paper really helps when planning out intarsia or Fair Isle designs. The websites below allow you to download and print off your own sheets, and the second option lets you input the exact tension of your knitting so that you produce a truly accurate representation of the finished knitting.

www.theknittingsite.com/knitting-graph-paper
www.tata-tatao.to/matrix/e-index.html
www.printablepaper.net/category/knitting